DON'T BE DISCOURAGED

by

Bert van Croonenburg, C.S.Sp.

DIMENSION BOOKS
Denville, New Jersey 07834

248. 2
✓

PUBLISHED BY DIMENSION BOOKS
Denville, New Jersey

Imprimi Potest:	Charles P. Connors, C.S.Sp.
	Provincial
Nihil Obstat:	William J. Winter, S.T.D.
	Censor Librorum
Imprimatur:	+ Vincent M. Leonard, D.D.
	Bishop of Pittsburgh
	November 20, 1972

The majority of souls are lost through discouragement.

Ven. Libermann.

Though the yield of the olive fail
and the terraces produce no nourishment
Though the flocks disappear from the fold
and there be no herd in the stalls
Yet will I rejoice in the Lord
and exult in my saving God.
God, my Lord, is my strength;
He makes my feet swift as those of hinds
and enables me to go upon the heights.

From the Lauds on Friday in Lent.

This book is not a complete study of the spiritual or religious life. It considers topics which regularly returned in my many conversations with religious sisters. As they judged these observations valuable, their requests to have them printed led to this publication.

Some of the ideas in this book have been inspired by the works and lectures of Adrian van Kaam, C.S.Sp., Ph.D. For that I owe him a debt of gratitude.

I am also grateful for the valuable suggestions he as well as Susan Muto, Ph.D. provided during the writing of this volume.

My sincere thanks to Sr. Celine Rachwal, S.D.R., M.A., who patiently and expertly typed the manuscript and corrected the proofs.

TABLE OF CONTENTS

TIME TO START

THE renewal of religious life started with the intention of making it more meaningful and appealing for our days. The result so far has been disappointing. The religious themselves seem rather confused about the meaning of their calling while for the average Catholic this vocation has become more meaningless. This lack of understanding may be one of the reasons why so few are attracted to the religious life.

Some see religious renewal as a failure. To us this seems a hasty and unjustified condemnation. We must not forget that although this renewal started more than ten years ago, it is far from finished. Fifty or a hundred years from now historians may recognize that this initial stage, with all its ups and downs, was a painful but necessary and healthy purification which brought religious life to greater vitality.

Although we cannot yet come to a final evaluation, it seems useful to survey the actual situation in order to see where we stand. Since we are so close to the events, a conclusive overview is not possible but several aspects can be indicated.

A new structure cannot be established successfully unless we have beforehand a plan and view of what we envision. Perhaps we have proceeded too hastily.

It is undeniable that before Vatican II religious life had become somewhat stagnated. Many agreed that it was out of touch with modern times and the attitude of contemporary man. The unfortunate fact is that few took the time or had the talent to find what were the fundamental defects. Most people limited themselves to what was amiss in the immediate external situation without properly examining the deeper roots.

Some thought there were too many regulations. Others were of the opinion that the recreational possibilities were insufficient. Common assistance at certain exercises was a source of irritation while the religious dress came in for a good amount of criticism. As long as all this was considered unchangeable there was little else to do than grimly bear it. But as soon as the signal for change was given there was a general assault on the various points of dissatisfaction. This was in itself quite normal and understandable but these points were unfortunately not considered against the background of the totality of religious life. They simply had to go. One gets the impression of people trying to fix their home. They spend money and effort to improve its inside and outside appearance but do not consider the possibility that the very foundation may have to be strengthened.

Besides this rather negative aspect, we see also positive factors. Emphasis has been restored to the value of one's personal responsibility and the respect of each one's individuality. It is true that some confused this emphasis with licence. Their mistake is perhaps the unavoidable companion of trying out the new orientation. Their misconception does not destroy the value of personal responsibility and unique individuality but invites us to proceed with greater caution.

Another gain of the renewal is the insight that not everything which came from the founders has to remain unchanged. Rules and customs which no longer have any meaning in our time should be abolished. In some instances we may have too hastily concluded to a lack of meaning but this does not invalidate the principle that certain rules and customs may have lost their meaning today.

Finally and most importantly, there is a growing awareness that true religious renewal requires more than just external changes. We see a longing for something deeper, something more meaningful, that can provide a foundation and center for the activities of everyday life. In other words, it seems that the time has come to start the inner, the *religious* renewal.

THE HEART OF THE MATTER

TO renew religious life we must clearly understand what religious life is. Without such insight we run the risk of eliminating what is essential while introducing what is harmful.

What does it mean to be a religious? To be a religious is not the same as being religious. In the latter case we only indicate a secondary characteristic. When I am called a religious this points to a typifying qualification. It brings out the central focus of my life and indicates that I have dedicated myself to make the living of religion my all-embracing concern and interest. It expresses the very substance of my daily living.

What does this living of religion mean? In order to clarify our thought, it seems useful to bring out first what the living of religion is not.

A first mistake is to identify the living of religion with the knowledge about God, be it philosophical or theological. This misunderstanding rests on the often tacit assumption that one's spirituality will increase in proportion to the growth of his philosophical and theological knowledge about God. We note here a fallacious identification of knowing and living. Studying God philosophically or theologically is an activity of the analytic mind which does not by itself engage the whole of man's living. Living religion is a total commitment to God that embraces one's thinking and willing as well as his doing.

To say it concretely, one with only rudimentary scientific knowledge about God can live a deep spiritual life. Witness are all those who without any philosophy and theology are fervent Christians. On the other hand, the spiritual depth of a theologian may be far behind his extensive knowledge of the divine mysteries.

In his book *Atheism in Our Time* Ignace Lepp tells us that in his college years he was an avowed atheist. He had to follow the regular schedule of courses which included philosophy of God. During the exam his examiner asked him to explain and elaborate the proofs for God's existence. He did so well that he received the highest grade. An avowed atheist could perfectly formulate the proofs which conclude to God's existence. A clear separation of knowing and living.

In the foregoing we in no way intend to deny that there is a close connection between the living of religion and the knowledge about God. Later on we shall elaborate on this close connection. All we want to emphasize here is that we should not identify the two. One who knows a great deal about God does not *by that fact itself* become a deeply religious person and one without any philosophical and theological study can live an authentic spiritual life.

Another mistake would be to identify the living of religion with social or charitable activity. Contemplative religious have little or nothing to show in the line of social or charitable involvement in the world. This does not prevent them from living a true spiritual life. Vatican II emphasized anew the great value of this life. Far from condemning their lack of social or charitable involvement in the world, the Church proposes them as an inspiration to the faithful.

Looking at this point from the other side, we certainly have met charitable workers and dedicated volunteers who do not believe in God. They give themselves generously out of purely humanistic motivations. In other words, these activities can be correctly performed by those who deny the basis of lived religion.

Here too we in no way deny the relationship between such activities and the living of religion. Our whole emphasis is on establishing that these two must not be identified. One who engages in social or charitable work does not *by that fact itself* become a spiritual person while one who lives a spiritual life can do so without being thus involved in the world.

Finally we must not identify the observance of law and custom with the living of religion. We all have heard during our formation years that holiness

[15]

consists in observing even the smallest point of our holy rule. None of us can forget the famous saying: "Keep the rule and the rule will keep you." From this saying it has sometimes been mistakenly concluded that observing law and custom is the same as the living of religion.

In the gospel Christ exhorts us to give alms, (Lk. 11, 41) but He also says: "When you give alms, do not have it trumpeted before you: this is what the hypocrites do in the synagogues and in the streets to win men's admiration. I tell you solemnly, they have had their reward. But when you give alms, your left hand must not know what your right hand is doing: your almsgiving must be in secret, and your Father who sees all that is done in secret will reward you" Mt. 6, 2-4. Almsgiving is not by itself an act pleasing to God. It can be abused by man to promote his own glory and thus be deprived of its religious value. This act becomes valuable in the spiritual realm only when it is done for the love and glory of God.

The same is valid for the observance of law and custom. When we were young, we all at times practiced this observance for a superficial reason. We hurried to be in time for fear of getting a bad mark. We kept our room neat to make a good impression. This attitude was encouraged by the fact that superiors too often used the observance of these external acts as the yardstick to evaluate the religious dimension of our lives.

Hopefully, when we grew up we realized that the depth of our spiritual life could not be measured by the mere observance of these acts but by the spirit that inspired and directed them. Unfortunately not all grow to this mature insight. Some continue to place the value of their life as religious mostly in the impression they make on their superiors. Their observance of law and custom serves mainly their self-enhancement in the eyes of others. Fundamentally their conduct resembles that of an atheist observing the law to avoid trouble.

Neither in this third point did we deny a relationship between the living of religion and the observance of custom and law. We only want to warn against the danger of identifying this observance with the living of religion.

We may now attempt to outline positively what the living of religion means. No religious living is possible for me unless I admit the reality of a transcendent being, a supreme source of existence. But this mere admission is not enough. One can accept the reality of the divine and live as if God did not exist. He cannot be said to live his religion. In order to come to the living of religion, it is necessary that God enters my everyday life not as an idea but as a person. On the other hand I have to become involved in relation to God. What does this mean: God has to enter my everyday life as a person and I have to get involved in relation to God.

I meet most people on what is called the object level. The janitor is just the janitor, that is not a person but a function. A bus driver is just a bus driver, a cashier is just a cashier. What in them is most important to me is not the person in his or her uniqueness but the function they perform. When this function is taken over by a machine, I may welcome the improvement and do not miss the person. The machine makes fewer mistakes anyhow.

Occasionally I meet the other person as a person. I discover her as a unique human being when she tells me of her miseries, her frustrations, her hopes. She is no longer an undistinguished entity absorbed in the mass of humanity. She stands before me in her uniqueness, totally unlike anyone else. She has manifested herself to me *as a person.*

This manifestation of the person is not the same as allowing her to enter my life. I once went to a store to buy a cigar holder. Below the counter I saw a whole collection. I told my desire to the saleslady and all she did was point to the exhibited holders. They were behind glass and I could not touch them. To my request to show me some, she replied, "Just tell me which one you want." I did not tell her. I had an unkind thought and walked away. I was standing before her with a specific wish, glad to have located finally a store that sold these holders. She on her part was not in the least interested either in the sale or in my wish. It is easy to condemn her but how often have I myself failed in this point? When someone told me her woes, I spoke some nice words without really being present to her. The person stood before me as a person but I did not allow her to enter my life.

Different is the situation when I really feel *with* and *for* the other person. This happens, for example, to those who as nurses are willing and able to listen with real concern to the already too well-known descriptions of their patients' pains. At this moment at least there is a communion of feeling. The patient knows she is not talking to a nursing machine but to a human being who feels with her and for her. The nurse allows the patient to enter her life and to a degree she gets involved in relation to the patient. She may say a few consoling words or straighten the bed to make her more comfortable.

We see here a two-sided interaction. The patient appeals to the interest and compassion of the nurse. She reveals her pains and miseries in order to be comforted and consoled. The nurse on her side tries to communicate to the patient that she cares. In other words, the nurse invests something of herself in the patient. She becomes involved in relation to her. No longer is she just a distributor of skill but a person who *as a person* is present to and gets involved in the patient.

The relationship between the nurse and the patient is only incidental. Every nurse knows that once the patient is cured she no longer belongs to the nursing world. She may occasionally drop in, but unless another personal bond develops each one will not miss the other and their involvement ceases.

Different is the situation when between two persons there is a lasting personal relationship. For example, I know a young mother who had her first baby about one year ago. She really cares for her baby. For his mother the little boy is never merely an object but a human being in which she is involved even when she sleeps. At the first cry of the baby she is awake. All this concern was not there two years ago but has come about since the child was conceived and even more since he was born. A person entered that woman's life and she became involved; she invested in this child all her life and care and concern.

In the other extreme we see a parallel when the relationship is one of deep personal hate. In olden times the six shooter brought a quick end to that hateful investment of the one in the other. Today we are more civilized and the process lasts much longer. There are persons who invest a great part of their lives in the attempt to destroy the other. Again a person has entered the other's life and the other has become involved in him in a personal though unfortunate way.

We may now try to find out what it means to allow God to enter my life as a person and to get involved in relation to Him. It is evident that though God is real He is not real for everyone. The divine is beyond the realm of the senses and those who limit their world to what the senses manifest eliminate even the possibility of openness to the Transcendent.

Because man is an incarnated spirit, he has the ability to go beyond the sense perceptible. This is not the same as allowing God to enter one's life. We talked before about Ignace Lepp, who in his youth was an avowed atheist. He faithfully studied his philosophy of God and he knew it so well that he passed his exam with the highest grade. Although his mind was occupied with the divine it was *only* his mind that was involved. He merely speculated concerning a concept to which according to him nothing corresponded in reality. This is why he could say he was an atheist. He denied the divine existence. God entered his life only as a concept and not as a person. Still less did he get involved in the divine.

Every human being sooner or later, and at various periods of his existence, is faced with the irruption of the divine in his life. This may be precipitated by an external event such as the sudden death of a close relative or the nearly miraculous escape in an airplane crash. At such a time man is faced with a dimension of life which he normally tries to hide from his attention. Unprepared he looks into an abyss which reaches beyond this world and makes the seemingly important things of his life seem shallow and secondary. Abruptly a crack appears in the map of life which he has so securely drawn. With this rupture comes an uncertainty concerning the meaning of life, its principles and goal.

A similar experience may come about through an inner psychological process such as, for example, adolescence. The young adolescent without fully knowing what is happening starts experiencing a terrifying loneliness. The world around him, his parents no longer seem to fit in his world. A hostility arises that estranges him still more. "They don't understand me" is the common complaint.

These feelings are a first sign of the struggle to come to selfhood. Only by being disengaged from the child's intimacy with the family can he hope to arrive at a personal stand in relation to values and persons. As the psychologists describe it, the world as well as the persons in it seem to recede from him. He has no contact with them anymore. He is left to himself. As he discovers his own self, he also becomes aware of his own responsibility. He realizes that he has to make his own way in life. He experiences his limitation but in this experience he reaches beyond it. For the first time in his life the young person as a person opens up to the Infinite. Somehow the mystery that is behind and in everything makes itself known as an important factor in his personal life. For the first time the young person as a person comes face to face with the divine.

When God enters the life of a person, He does this not by forcing Himself upon him but by way of appeal. His is an invitation to trust in Him and to surrender to Him. The infinite love seeks from man a free answer.

With no compulsion on the part of God, man is always able to refuse. But even if he answers this first appeal, his is not yet true religious living. In this first surrender man has invested something of himself in God but this can be merely a transitory experience. We see a parallel in the nurse who, when she is in a good mood, is willing to be kind and compassionate to her patients. This attitude is just a passing event and not a permanent characteristic of her whole life. One who occasionally has pious thoughts does not yet truly live religion.

The love of a mother for her child, by contrast, is not something that comes and goes. It is a permanent vital element of her everyday existence and permeates her whole life. In a similar way I truly live my religion when openness and surrender to the divine become a permanent attitude, an all-pervading reality of my being.

The living of religion is not a once and for all operation. Neither is my surrender to God something which I give at one moment while at another moment I withdraw it. I surrender to God precisely because

He is God, the One on whom I depend every instant of my life and who in all the aspects of my life has to be my goal and orientation. The living of religion, then, is only possible when there is in me a continuous attitude of surrender to God. This attitude starts with one simple act. As time goes by, it becomes a deepened, spontaneous, stable and all-permeating orientation of my life.

In the beginning of man's personal contact with God, he is normally impressed by the majesty of the divine as well as by his own total dependence upon God. He surrenders mostly out of fear. This is not wrong in itself but unless a further development takes place it is probable that sooner or later he will withdraw his surrender. When a concrete temptation comes, the allurement of what is forbidden is *now* strongly appealing while hell seems far.

As man grows in intimacy with the divine, there emerges a new sound and a new dimension in this person to person relationship with God. The more man becomes open to the divine and is penetrated by His presence, the more he realizes that this appeal by God is given not merely because He wants to show His power. Slowly, but increasingly, man discovers that the appeal to surrender comes from God's infinite love for man, for the good of man himself. Only in and through this surrender can man reach his true happiness. This is the aim of any religion that has developed a true view of God.

In Christian religion this divine care finds its climax in the redeeming Christ. In His sacrifice He undeniably manifests His infinite love for man by investing His life in man's redemption in order to open the way to heaven. Once man becomes vitally aware that the appeal from the divine is an invitation from infinite, unselfish, dedicated love, he also experiences that surrender is asked of him not merely because there is no other way out. Rather the advances of divine love can be properly met only with a surrender in and out of love. He loves me so much that even when I was a sinner, His enemy in the realm of grace, He gave His life for me. Such a love has no other appropriate response than a total surrender in love, a surrender that makes God the center of my existence, the permanent goal to which my whole life and all my activities are oriented.

Human life is not a static entity but a reality growing in always new dimensions. Coming to the United States in 1952 from the quiet life of a seminary professor, I entered the bustling world of an urban university. I had to learn to face and to be present to a new mentality, a new way of living, new cultural experiences. This is a never ending process. I saw a gradual change from the neat young students of 1952 to the rather raggy crowd of today. This exterior change is accompanied by a constant development of new ideas, interest, behavior. Culture is always on the move. We all have to face this development in our work. How much different is the modern math from the one you learned when you were a student? How many new methods of teaching have been introduced since you started teaching? How many new practices have you seen in treating patients and organizing hospital care? Our world of meaning is constantly expanding and changing in a movement of differentiation.

This movement of differentiation is disturbing. We can never say, "I have arrived." Once I have come to a certain presence and attitude in relation to my work and my surroundings, new elements require again a process of adjustment. I have to give these new elements their proper place in the totality of my life or I become spread out and chaotic. The movement of differentiation has to be counteracted by another basic human movement, that of integration. Only when I live an integrated life can I come to the maturity and wholeness which are required for sound human living.

These two movements, differentiation and integration, have to be present simultaneously in a healthy human life. If one refuses any further differentiation, he becomes stagnated, stifled and anxious. He must constantly defend himself against oncoming new perspectives and realities. If the movement of integration is lacking, a person becomes confused and the way is open to psychological difficulties.

Differentiation upsets the balance of our lives. We have to cope with something new to which we are not accustomed. This is always painful but inevitable and necessary to human growth. When a young woman falls in love for the first time a whole new factor enters her life. The glowing feeling of love is present the entire day. It is so absorbingly experienced that it is difficult to be with other persons than the beloved. Study and work suffer because she is not really with it. This new experience pushes all the rest to the background and occupies the totality of her life. Only through the movement of integration can it be brought back to its proper place in everyday life.

Integration presupposes in my life a hierarchy of values. In this hierarchy our values are ordered in relation to a central one which unites and orients all the others in appropriate subordination.

There are people whose unifying principle in life is money. That is their only interest and security. Whatever they see is evaluated in dollars and cents. Some live only for their family. They work and slave to provide a good home and an excellent education for their children. The good of their family is their central motivating force. For others God is the central value. Their life is an answer to the invitation of divine love. Whatever comes to them is considered a gift from God to help them become what He wants them to be.

For most people this divine love becomes the background of their professional and family life. It gives richness and depth to all they do. Whomever they meet they face them as persons loved by God and redeemed by Him. Some have become so overwhelmed by the divine love that the answer to this love is their primary occupation. They are the ones who by God's calling and their free consent to this call have become religious. God is the central all-embracing reality in their life and through their union with Him they see world and man as His manifestation. But such a life is possible only when they face God as God.

When I was in the novitiate we had, after two and a half months, our first big retreat of eight full days. That retreat was called the conversion retreat. This seemed a strange name since the retreat was given to young men who had already spent six years in the junior seminary trying to live a good Christian life. Stranger still was the material given in the conferences as subject for our meditation. The master of novices took as his first topic the creation. He showed how Adam and Eve sinned and thus affected the whole human race. Then quietly and skillfully we were made aware that in spite of our great ideas (we were after all young men who had just finished their secondary studies) we were only zeros. We existed only because God in His continuing creative act maintained us in existence out of pure goodness. In spite of all the graces and favors bestowed on us, we were often unfaithful to God.

The whole retreat had only one intent: to make us clearly aware that we did not give existence to ourselves and that of ourselves we were nothing but sinners. That we existed was not our doing but God's. That we were in the state of grace and friendship with God was not due to our cleverness or ability but solely to the merciful kindness of the redeeming Christ. In answer to all this we sinned. After eight full days of this, we could not help but feel dirty and were only too willing to make a general confession to get rid of our sins.

When I myself made this retreat, I did not ask why we had to go through this experience. I only realized that it was not very pleasant. Entering the novitiate I thought myself pretty good. I was successful in my studies and thought myself rather wise and mature. Spiritually too I had not done so badly. Then suddenly I was brought down from my pedestal. I had to face the fact that when all was said and done I was phony.

Reflecting on this retreat after a number of years, I

see now that this whole procedure was wise and meaningful. Only after painfully living through this experience was I able to face God as God.

Religious living is only possible when God enters my life as a person and not merely as an idea. Individually I have to come face to face with the person who is God. I have, moreover, to become involved and to surrender to Him so that he really can become the all-pervading and permeating center and orientation of my life.

In this person to person encounter with the divine much depends on my individual attitude. God is unchangeably the same but the way I allow Him to invade me and to become a reality in my life depends on the personal attitude I bring to this encounter. We see this dependence already in the human relationships. If I am of a suspicious nature, I don't trust even a kind person. The more she is kind the more perhaps I distrust her. "She is so kind, she must want something." If on the other hand I am an understanding and open person, I find some good even in an unattractive neighbor. "She is unbearable but . . ."

Similarly, when God enters my life as a person, I am there with my specific character structure, my mood, my basic psychological attitude, my pride. On the path of our spiritual progress have we not all fallen into the trap of pride? Do you remember the earlier months of your novitiate? If you had a good novitiate, you noticed that after some time you were doing rather well. Then you happened to meet a sister (an older one) who gossiped, who did not observe silence, who criticized the superior. And the spontaneous thought came "Thank God that I am better than she." That "Thank God" was only to make it sound pious. Deep in your heart you were convinced that you were holier. Though you did not say it, in the secret recesses of your heart you attributed to yourself and to your own effort and power the fact that you were so good. You appropriated to yourself what was possible solely because of God's grace in spite of your infidelities and faults. The sin of pride! A sin so subtle that it is a threat to even the holiest person.

I only face God as God when I am vividly aware that I am a creature, that I exist every moment through His loving and sustaining providence which keeps me in existence.

I only face God as God when I am deeply aware that I am a sinner in constant need of redemption.

I only face God as God when I have a lived conviction that without His graces, of many kinds, given gratuitously and in spite of my infidelity, I would be in enmity with Him. When, with these words, I feel a twinge of unpleasantness, it shows that I still do not want to accept that in the order of grace I am what I am only through His mercy.

I only face God as God when I have an unlimited trust in His infinite love and learn to accept *whatever He sends* in full submission and without question.

The call to face God as God makes heavy demands. If you want to find out how difficult the answer to this call is, you should some day take time out of your busy schedule. Place yourself before God just as you do when you make your meditation. Talk to Him as simply as you can. Tell Him that you love Him because He loves you and gave His life to save you, that you really are convinced that His infinite love wants nothing but the best for you. Trusting in His mercy and kindness you hope that He will give you the graces necessary for salvation. You may thank Him for all the benefits you have received in the realm of grace but also in the area of daily living, such as good health and perhaps even success.

It would be quite normal to ask Him to continue to grant you these and similar favors. All this is quite simple and not difficult because all what you have said does not demand any sacrifice. But you should go further.

If you really are convinced that whatever His love sends you is for your good and a gift of love, you will also sincerely thank Him for the headache that bothers you, for the arthritis that is so painful, for the spiritual darkness which now for months already has enveloped you. "We accept good things from God; and should we not accept evil?" Job 2, 10. This of course will not prevent you from asking that these woes be taken away, but as He knows best what is good for you, you should also thank Him beforehand in case He does not see fit to make an end to these miseries.

You surrender because of your confidence in His infinite love and wisdom. Refusing to submit in any specific point is placing yourself above Him. You do not face God as God. You act as if you know better and thus degrade Him. You have not fully surrendered to God.

But even that is not enough. I know a man who in a generous mood gave to a good cause all the money he had in his pocket but kept a few quarters. "You never know what will happen," was his excuse. He did not really give *all* his money.

We often have this same attitude toward God and thus we fall short of true surrender. Really surrendering to God implies to hand over everything, to give Him a free hand in relation to your present as well as your future. You trust Him in the full sense only when you allow Him *to direct your life to whatever goal He wishes and in whatever way He chooses without any reservation or restriction on your part.* Without giving Him this "carte blanche" you do not really trust Him or surrender to Him. You then do not face God as God, as the infinitely trustworthy and caring One.

You should not stop half way. You must certainly

thank Him for all the favors He has given. You should also thank Him for the unpleasant things, since they too are a sign of His love. But you must go still a step further. If you are really convinced that He wants only what is good for you, you must allow Him to do with you *whatever* He wants. This does not exclude the fact that you express your preferences and that you implore Him to avert from you what is painful. But always you should add that if He decides otherwise you will then too thank Him wholeheartedly. In surrendering to God you have to go all the way or you do not really surrender nor do you fully trust Him. You do not face God as God.

Why is this total surrender so difficult? Voluntary surrender implies trust in the one to whom I surrender. When I use a plane I surrender my life to the pilot. I trust that he will bring me to my destination so that we do not land where there is no airfield or on the wrong airfield. The fact that I rely on this man in piloting the plane does not mean that I trust him with a million dollars. That money I bring to the bank, with the confidence that the banker will take proper care of it. While in bank operations the banker is qualified, I do not ask him to fly me to my destination. Among men, we trust the other only in the field for which he is qualified. Even that implies a risk.

When I read in the paper that a bank goes bankrupt, I realize that banking my money involves a risk. It is risk which I can take because it is relatively small. Normally banks take good care of the money entrusted to them. Similarly, though all pilots get their regular physical check up, it happens occasionally that a pilot gets a heart attack. The co-pilot has to take the plane down by himself with perhaps less experience. Who knows what is going to happen? Nevertheless, boarding a plane, I don't worry about the health of the pilots. In both our examples there is a certain risk which I can gage. Normally I don't worry about it.

The willingness to surrender and to trust the other diminishes in proportion with the increase of the risk involved. Suppose a balloonist invites me for a balloon ride. I know he is very qualified . . . though twice he got hung up in the top of a high tree and three times he landed in water. I have never been in a balloon. I am not acquainted with all that flying in it involves. It is now much harder for me to measure the risk than when I fly on a regular plane. I am not sure I would accept his invitation.

Worse is the situation when a racer needs a second man for his side car. I never sat in a side car. All I know of them is what I have seen in the movies where the riders in the side car hang mostly outside the car to counterbalance the weight in the turns. Here is a risk I am totally unable to gage. I am sure that I shall as kindly as possible decline the offer even if it gives me half of the first prize.

A similar thing happens in our total surrender to the divine love. We love Him. We trust His infinite love. We are sure that He will help us. All these elements do not eliminate the fact that when I surrender to Him all the facets of my life, I engage myself far beyond what I am able to foresee. This unconditional engagement makes it so difficult to surrender *totally* to God.

We are children of a culture that emphasizes that we have to be on top of things. This total surrender asks us to commit ourselves without seeing where it will bring us and without the ability to evaluate all that it involves. No wonder it evokes in us a spontaneous resistance which is not so easily overcome.

Nevertheless, only when I totally surrender to the wise and caring love of God, only when I give Him an absolutely free hand, only when I give Him total credit without any restriction do I face God as God, do I allow Him to be God for me.

This is often called the leap in the dark. There is darkness insofar as I do not see where and what it will bring me. On the other hand, it is clear to me in faith that it is a leap into the security of God's love. Through this leap I actually start following Christ whose leading theme of life was "Father, let your will be done, not mine" Lk. 22, 42. Its echo is found in the words of our Blessed Mother, "Be it done to me according to your word" Lk. 1, 38.

In this total surrender we answer the infinite love of God with the full potential of our human love, which is the only answer worthy of the divine. We are intent upon pleasing the Beloved by giving ourselves to Him without holding anything back. Our whole life then becomes oriented to the One who gave His life for us. We truly face God as God and in the full sense we are living our religion.

We must now return to the erroneous views of religion we examined earlier. We saw that we should not identify the living of religion with philosophical or theological knowledge about God. This knowledge can be a purely intellectual pursuit. It is possible that one fills his mind with ideas of the divine while God, the reality, does not enter his life and he himself in no way gets involved in God. On the other hand, we said, there is a relation between the living of religion and the knowledge about God. One who in total surrender of love fundamentally invests his life in the divine, will certainly, within the realm of his possibility, attempt to acquire more knowledge about the Beloved. This knowledge pursued and assimilated in love can in turn bring God closer to him and thus in a circular movement increase his love for God. It seems unthinkable that one who faces God as God in love can remain indifferent in relation to an increased knowledge of the divine. His very love will stimulate him according to his ability to know the Beloved better precisely in order to love Him more intensely.

We also mentioned that it would be a mistake to identify the living of religion with social or charitable activities. But, when in total dedication of love we face God as God, we cannot remain indifferent toward our fellowmen, who are also the object of the divine goodness and redeemed by Christ. Living religion means opening up to the divine life that through grace is given to us. Closing our hearts to our neighbor is closing ourselves to that divine life which in its infinite care embraces all men and desires to bring them to salvation. As St. John says in his first letter (4, 7-12):

> "My dear people,
> let us love one another
> since love comes from God
> and everyone who loves is begotten by God and knows God.
> Anyone who fails to love can never have known God,
> because God is love.
> God's love for us was revealed
> when God sent into the world his only Son
> so that we could have life through him;
> this is the love I mean:
> not our love for God,
> but God's love for us when he sent his Son
> to be the sacrifice that takes our sins away.
> My dear people,
> since God has loved us so much
> we too should love one another.

No one has ever seen God;
but as long as we love one another
God will live in us
and his love will be complete in us."

There is then an undeniable link between the living of religion and doing good to our fellow men in accordance with our actual situation.

As a third point we made clear that we must not identify the living of religion with the observance of law or custom. One who observes the rules and regulations merely to look good or to avoid punishment can do so without any religious sentiment or dedication. On the other hand, one who sincerely, in a total surrender of love, allows God to enter his life as a person, intimately lives the fact that God in His love orders everything to the good of man. He will see the tender care of God in the daily circumstances of life among which are rules and regulations. These rules and regulations become windows upon God. The very love for God will urge the religious person to observe them to the best of his ability.

Concluding we must say that these various fields must not be identified with the living of religion but are closely connected with it. They are the realm in which man's love for God flows over and becomes incarnated. Unless one's love for God radiates actively into these fields, insofar as his condition allows, such a person cannot be said to truly love God nor to live his religion.

TO be a religious is to make the living of religion my primary concern. I allow God to enter my life as a person and I become involved in Him in such a way that He is the orientation and goal of all aspects of my life.

I entered religious life in answer to the divine call which invited me to live in the intimacy of love with God. In unselfish surrender and dedication, I attempt to answer His love to the full potential of my ability in nature and grace. By sacrificing self-centeredness and egoistic desires I start living a God-centered life of grace. "Anyone who finds his life will lose it; anyone who loses his life for my sake will find it" Mt. 10, 39. "If anyone loves me he will keep my word, and my Father will love him, and we shall come to him and make our home with him" John 4, 23. This intimacy with God brings growing sanctification and sets me on the path to heaven. Following the divine call to religious life I save my soul.

The desire to save one's soul and to bring glory to God was in the past for many a sufficient reason to enter the convent or monastery. But our outlook has changed. We have become more clearly aware that no man can be concerned only with himself and least of all in the spiritual realm. We are social beings with a social responsibility. It is, therefore, important to examine the value and meaning of religious life in relation to the totality of our culture.

Culture today is quite complex. There are many values which help man to grow and develop. This growth and development is properly taken care of when all the important dimensions are sufficiently attended to. Not all elements are of equal importance but if some fundamental value is overlooked the culture as a whole becomes stunted.

What causes a specific point to be properly taken care of or to become neglected? At present we are very health conscious. Practically everyone speaks about vitamins, carbohydrates, cholesterol, calories and whatever other medical terms are the fad of the day. This health consciousness does not come about by itself. First the drug manufacturers bring to man's attention various aches and pains that may bother him. Backache, headache, arthritis pain, upset stomach, psoriasis, tired blood, iron deficiency. These are only a few of the items on the long list of human woes of which we are constantly made aware along with, of course, the proper remedy. Public health officials add their voice to this chorus. Cigarette smoking is dangerous; fish may be mercury contaminated; smog is a health hazard; car exhausts are dangerous; check regularly for cancer symptoms, and so on. No one in our society can be ignorant of the value of health and the many threats to it. The medical profession aided by the officials as well as by the drug manufacturers communicate a constant stream of information and warnings which no one can escape or ignore. Together they form a powerful center that radiates health awareness and care. This value radiation center makes the people not only know more about health but also take better care of it.[1]

What we say here about health awareness is valid also for other factors. Thus, for example, we have all become pollution conscious because of the recent concentrated effort to improve our environment.

As long as a value radiation center remains active and dynamic the population at large can remain informed about that value and incorporate it in daily thinking and living. If, however, such a center slackens its activity, it is more than probable that the value it stands for will lose its importance for the population. This value may then be relegated to the background or even be lost. Suppose that from now

---

[1] The theory of culture as a field of centers of value radiation was taken from Adrian van Kaam, C.S.Sp., Ph.D. Those who want to study this theory more extensively we refer to the following works of this author: *Personality Fulfillment in the Religious Life* (Denville, N.J.: Dimension Books, Inc., 1967); *The Vowed Life* (Denville, N.J.: Dimension Books, Inc., 1968); *Envy and Originality* (Garden City, N.Y.: Doubleday & Company, 1972).

on no doctor, no article, no communication ever brought out that cigarette smoking may be harmful to one's health. A few years from now this danger will be practically overlooked.

It is important then that a value radiation center remain active and dynamic. This does not mean that such a center will succeed in influencing the population as a whole. History shows that a value which comes to the fore in one era may be forgotten in a later one. The renaissance for example discovered classical civilization. Through the activity of the classicists, Greek and Latin came to be considered necessary for a true education. As science and technique acquired greater interest the importance of classical studies decreased. At present the Greek and Roman culture are still considered valuable in the historical sense but few look at them as a worthwhile part of man's education. Those who never studied the classics do not experience this as a handicap or a lacuna.

It is important to realize that when a certain aspect of the culture declines in acceptance, the value radiation center does not become less but more necessary. As long as everyone cherishes a cultural element, it is not in danger of being neglected. Precisely when the general interest goes down the value radiation center is more urgently needed. It may be the only place where this value is lived and handed down. When, at a later period, the population as a whole again awakens to its importance, it will be thanks to the radiation center that this value did not get totally lost but is available for those who are open to it. This safeguarding is all the more necessary when the factor in question is more central to the culture.

Such a period of decline is always painful to those who highly estimate a certain facet of the culture. They decry this disregard but often fail to see that it contains also a valuable dimension. As long as a value is popular it attracts many who cultivate it not because they see it as precious but because it is the "in" thing. Suppose that painting grows to a highly regarded cultural expression. It becomes a haven then not only for true artists but also for those who see in it a road to fame and riches. They give themselves to painting not because of an inner calling but as a means of prestige. As soon as this money-making possibility declines they turn to something else that provides better economic and social prospects. Thus the artistic world is freed from the followers who were not truly interested in painting as an expression of beauty. Only those truly devoted to this art will go on in spite of the hardships this entails. In this sense, a period of decline serves as a salutary test of the intention of those who give themselves to a cultural aspect.

In this light we can understand our calling to the religious life. The transcendent dimension, that openness to the divine, is the culminating point as well as the center of all cultural development. Only when the culture is anchored in this central value can it grow harmoniously and be a true contribution to the authentic development of mankind. Without this transcendent openness man becomes chained to the secondary values and estranged from his true self; he can never come to authentic self-realization. The religious dimension is a fundamental factor without which man cannot reach the destiny to which he is called.

In archaic society relatively few things were known and everyone could absorb and handle them all. The various cultural aspects were harmoniously united so that none of them was over-emphasized at the cost of the others. This balance became difficult when the culture increased in complexity. No one man could any longer fully master the various facets. Each one according to his inclination followed a certain specialization. Value radiation centers which made their specific value available to all came into existence.

Thus long before Christ we see people who by inclination and calling center their life on the transcendent dimension of reality. They make being and living with the divine their primary concern and form a radiation center of the spiritual values. Through their activity and inspiration the average man was reminded that he too was called to this intimacy with God.

Here also it is true that the more the culture is in

danger of forgetting its transcendent calling the more such a spiritual radiation center is needed to safeguard against a total loss. We, the religious, are by divine calling destined to radiate what we ourselves live. We have to show others that the living of religion is not only fundamental to their true happiness but also that this total surrender of love to God is possible and salutary. For that we have to witness in our personal daily life.

This witnessing for spiritual life may at times seem a rather sterile effort. Interest in religion has been declining. In the past a regular influx of new candidates strengthened the ranks but at present few apply for admission. At the same time a number with temporary or perpetual vows are leaving. Apparently the many thousands of religious do not make much of an impact on the population as a whole. Even in their own ranks we see discouragement and confusion about the meaningfulness of their life.

The danger is that out of a sense of perhaps unconscious frustration some try to make an impact on the world in realms other than the living of religion. They see their chance in social care, integration, women's liberation, etc. There is, of course, no objection against religious entering these various fields as long as this is compatible with their religious life in a specific order in a concrete situation. The temptation, however, is great to *substitute* these activities for the witnessing for religion. We must never forget that the main concern of religious life is centering ourselves on the intimacy with God and witnessing in the world for the possibility, the beauty and the joy of this way of life. We have not entered the convent or monastery to witness for better social or political conditions but to witness for spiritual values. This witnessing does not exclude activity in other fields but this activity must be the overflow and the incarnation of our personal surrender to God. Only then is it possible to take part in the culture in such a way that our daily task becomes a witnessing, a manifestation of and an invitation to the love for God.

We must not be discouraged when at present our witnessing is that of a voice calling in the desert. The center of spiritual value radiation is not less important when its message is not heeded. On the contrary, it is all the more necessary to safeguard the transcendent dimension for the time when the culture turns again to its spiritual center.

We must consider such a time of decline as an invitation to purify ourselves. Perhaps when we entered it was considered a very honorable decision. Though the high esteem we gained was not our main motive, we derived no doubt a great deal of satisfaction from it. In our days we may have to do without these gratifications. This changed cultural attitude offers us a greater possibility of unselfishly making God the center of our dedication and love. We are cleansed from self-centered motives and able to live for the divine with fewer obstacles. As others seem to neglect the divine worship, we must in our life increase the attempt to honor and glorify Him and to atone for those who do not accept His love. The more we purify our personel love and unselfish dedication, the better we shall be able to bear witness for the living of religion.

We must not confuse bearing witness and making a statement of observation. When I state that water boils at 212 degrees, I communicate a fact which in no way involves me personally. I would not feel better or worse if water boiled at 180 or 367 degrees. In other words, when making a statement of observation, I communicate something that is outside my actual life process. In a similar way, when I declare that Napoleon died in 1821, this is nothing to get excited about. It is a mere fact of which I have taken cognizance but for the rest it does not affect my personal life in any way. If he had died in 1854 or 1832, it would not change one iota of my existence because it has nothing to do with my personal way of living.

Different is the situation when we speak about witnessing. Walking peacefully in a street I become aware that a lady on the fifth floor comes to the window with a flowerpot in her hands. She blows the dust from the plant and takes out some dead flowers. Suddenly the pot slips through her hands and falls into the street just missing a man's head. The man screams, looks up and sees nobody. I approach and tell him what I saw. His ire increases. "That woman on the fifth floor! She hates me, she wants to kill me." Suppose he sues her. As I am the only one who saw the accident, I am called to testify, to be a witness. I can only tell what I myself saw, that is what has become part of my personal experience.

In court the judge may ask: "Did the lady look down before she dropped the flowerpot?" "I did not see her look down. From where I walked she seemed totally absorbed in her plant." "What did she do when the pot fell?" "Her hands went up as in amazement and then she looked down." "What did she do further?" "I don't know. From that moment on I followed the pot with my eyes and scanned the street to see if anyone was close by, but before I could give any alarm the flowerpot reached the street."

In giving witness it was not important what I thought or what I had read but only and exclusively what I myself had experienced. Only to that could I testify and to nothing more. The whole value of my testimony rests upon my personal experience and upon my stating of that experience. Witnessing, then, or bearing witness always refers to that which I know through personal experience.

As religious we are called to witness for living in

intimacy with God and for the possibility, beauty and joy of this person to person relationship with the divine. This means that we can truly witness only if we ourselves live this transcendent dimension so that it has become part of our personal experience. As long as we ourselves have not become involved in God in our personal life we cannot testify for it.

Why should we bear witness of this spiritual living and not merely make a statement of observation about it? It is to be remembered that we as religious are the guardians of spiritual values for the whole culture. We must show the way so that others in turn will attempt to live this intimacy with the divine in their own life and situation. We are to safeguard and to communicate not just some intellectual insight but a *way of living*. Only by ourselves *living* this spiritual dimension can we convince others that they too can live this life of religion.

A Dutch proverb says that words demand attention but that examples make followers. Only by actually living this life shall we be able to manifest to others its true value and meaning. With the grace of God they in their turn may attempt to make this intimacy with God a part of their daily *living*.

Embracing the religious life is assuming the obligation to make the living of religion a reality in my personal living, that is to make it *really* the center of my existence and the central goal of all my striving.

Refusing or neglecting to do this is to refuse or neglect the heart and core of my religious vocation and it disqualifies me as a witness for religion.

Though all religious are called to be witnesses for the living of religion, they do not all do this in the same way.

There is first the contemplative religious. As we have seen, the heart and the core of all religious life is the living intimacy in a person to person relationship with God. This is the central value to which all others become secondary. If any other value threatens to become an obstacle, it must as far as possible be eliminated. To understand at least something concerning the contemplative life, we must be vitally aware of this center. We must realize that for every religious God is not a phantasy or merely a concept. He is as real and, in a certain sense, more real to them than any other reality. Only in this perspective can we understand that the surrender to God is not a mere formula but a personal answer to infinite love. It is a true consecration to God who again is not an idea but a true reality. Keeping in mind this true actuality of the divine love, it becomes understandable that a religious makes this loving surrender the highest goal, the center and core of her existence.

This personal interaction between man and God

takes place in our inner depth. However, we are not pure spirits but incarnated spirits. We are also our body. Through its senses, we become involved in the world beyond our body. Everyone who has attempted to be present to the divine in his inner depth knows by experience that in order to live the spiritual life, he has to learn to disengage himself from the external world. We do not say that he has to deny this external world. This would lead to repression with all the consequent psychological difficulties. Man has to disengage himself so that the external world does not overwhelm him. If he becomes tied down within it, his openness to the divine will be suffocated.

The contemplative religious, when entering the monastery, makes a radical decision. By God's call and aided by His grace, she eliminates from her life at once many of the obstacles to a life of deep spirituality so as to be more free to give herself to intimacy with God. This is a fundamental decision which should not be taken lightly. Not everyone is called or able to live such a life. Once we ourselves have come to a deeply lived awareness of the reality of God's immense love, we can understand that there are persons who can make this radical decision in order to more fully concentrate on this union with God.

To a number of people this appears as selfishness and a kind of spiritual gluttony. What good after all

do these persons do to the world, and more concretely to me? Anyone acquainted with the spiritual life
knows that living in intimacy with God is just the
opposite of selfishness. It is only to the degree that
one renounces self that she allows God to take
possession of her. This renouncement of self is not an
easy task.

The venerable Libermann writes to one of his
disciples: "Don't imagine that Jesus' divine and
adorable will is soon to win complete and perfect
mastery over you. Time will be needed, struggles,
crosses, miseries, much obscurity, renunciations and
humiliations" *Letters,* Vol. V, p. 182. This litany,
small though it be, shows at what cost union with
God is to be obtained.

What value is such a life to the world? To answer
this question we must not approach it from any
preconceived idea. Only in the light of faith can we
discern the true value and meaning of the contemplative life. We must forsake the notion that true
happiness in this world can be reached by human
means, by the progress and the tools of science and
economy. It is beyond doubt that modern comfort
and facilities contribute greatly in eliminating many
hardships. But by themselves they do not reach the
spiritual level where alone can be found the true
happiness that lasts through all situations of life.
"What gain, then, is it for a man to have won the

whole world and to have lost or ruined his very self?"
Lk. 9, 25.

Only through the grace and assistance of God does
one make her life meaningful and save her very self.
We all know this truth and quite possibly have many
times formulated it ourselves. Nevertheless, it becomes truly *meaningful* to me only when I myself
have deeply experienced my total inability on the
supernatural level when left to my own devices. When
I myself have agonized through this incapacity to save
my soul through my own power, do I realize that the
truest benefactors of mankind are not the technicians
and engineers, not the politicians and manufacturers,
not the organizers and statisticians but those who
through an intense spiritual life, through their prayers
and suffering obtain for the world God's grace, the
only source of man's lasting growth and happiness.

It is in this light of faith that we have to search for
the answer to the question: what good do the
contemplatives do to the world? The contemplative
has radically eliminated a number of obstacles to a
deep spiritual life. In order to be more free for the
living of God's intimacy, she freely has limited her
external world to that space within the enclosure.
This does not mean that she is no longer concerned
with the world beyond the enclosure. The contemplative enters the monastery not in order to get rid of
the world but to find it in the right way. It is not her

intention to have nothing to do with the world but to attempt in a concentrated way to do it the most good.

The core of religious life is the concentration on the interaction of love with the divine. But the divine is Christ the Redeemer, Christ who gave His life with the purpose of bringing *all* men to union with the Father. Anyone who has seriously meditated on the suffering of Christ cannot but suffer from the appalling incongruity that such a total immolation is still not known to or ignored by so many. St. Francis' crying because the world does not love God is not just a pious story but the accentuation of a compassion with Christ that is experienced by all who sincerely love Him. It is impossible to be truly dedicated to Christ and to be indifferent to the world He came to redeem.

The contemplative stands at the very center of the mystery of redemption where the contemplation of the Redeemer necessarily implies those to be redeemed; vice versa, meditation on those in need of redemption inevitably brings the Redeemer in focus. The contemplative life, then, as all spiritual life is not a schizoid existence but a uniting of facets which outside this realm are faced as disjointed.

This yearning and suffering with Christ for the redemption of the world is not a futile gesture. St. Paul writes to the Colossians 1, 24: "It makes me happy to suffer for you, as I am suffering now, and in

my body to do what I can to make up all that has still
to be undergone by Christ for the sake of his body,
the Church." Christ in His physical body once and for
all completed His suffering and went to His Father.
The mystical Christ, that body of all the faithful of
which Christ is the head, has still to go through much
suffering so that the fruit of Christ's passion may be
given to many.

The contemplative who fully dedicates her life to
intimacy with God does so out of love for Christ and,
because of her love for Christ, also out of love for
those to be redeemed. It is this love for Christ and the
souls to be redeemed that gives her the courage to
face the anxiety, darkness, suffering and crosses which
are inevitably connected with this sharing in the work
of redemption. Thus the contemplative monasteries
become the powerhouses of the Church, for through
their suffering and love grace and strength are more
abundantly given to a sick world. These religious do
not make the headlines, their names are mostly
unknown and they are hardly ever mentioned, but if
the world is saved from spiritual disaster it is certain
that these true benefactors of mankind have played
an important role.

If the contemplatives are hardly ever mentioned,
how can they be said to be witnesses in the world?
How can they give testimony in the world when they
never leave their enclosure and very few are allowed
to talk to them? The answer is paradoxical but we

must say that they witness for the value of spiritual living *precisely because they do not leave the enclosure.*

Until a few years ago I had never visited a contemplative monastery. I always greatly admired these people and from what I knew I was convinced that their life was of great value to the Church. Then I was invited to stay for one month in a monastery of contemplative sisters. From my limited contact with them I became more impressed and edified and also more convinced of the beauty of their life. Still I had not yet a clear insight in what way they were important as witnesses who testified to the world about the value of spiritual living. The answer to this question was given by the people I met there.

The monastery was outside a little village. People from all classes, from all ages and from all faiths came to visit the place. During the weekdays the traffic normally was only a trickle. Over the weekends, however, one car after another stopped, people came out, visited the church and left again. At certain hours they could hear the nuns singing behind the grill or saying the office. At other times they simply looked at those grills behind which curtains blocked any further view. It puzzled me. What did they come for and what was their impression? I started, therefore, talking to them, ready to answer their inquiries. It was then that I got the answer to my question, an answer that because of its very simplicity had escaped

me. What they communicated to me came to this:
"Isn't that something? People leaving everything else
just to be able to live for God and love Him. They
must really mean it. I don't know how they can do it
but they take this thing of God really seriously. Never
to leave this enclosure and all that praying and
fasting. You know, it makes you think and look at
your own life." These thoughts, formulated by
hippies, well-to-do persons and people just on the go,
brought home to me more clearly the witness value of
the contemplative life than any book. We too often
forget that the strongest testimony is not given by
words but by just simply and faithfully living the
value we stand for. What we *are* counts much more
than what we say.

Another way of witnessing for the living of religion
is practiced by the participative religious. For them
too lived union with God is the center and core of
their lives. They too have fully surrendered to the
divine love and have made this surrender the highest
in their hierarchy of values. But where the contemplative has, so to speak, withdrawn into the desert to
fight in solitude the life long battle of bringing her
will in union with the divine will, the participative
religious remains in the middle of the arena that is the
world. Her witnessing takes place in the hospital, the

school, the social center, the old folks home, the nursery. Though this way of living does not know some of the hardships the contemplative faces, it must be admitted that in the spiritual realm the participative religious life contains special difficulties. Its contact with the divine is more tenuous. The contemplative freely limits her external world to the space within the enclosure. Thus she leaves behind a number of the obstacles that threaten the development of true spirituality. The participative religious has not been so fortunate. She lives in the world with its dangers. It is precisely in the midst of this concrete situation that she must witness to the world. She must sanctify the daily struggle by making these very obstacles means of growing intimacy and union with God.

It cannot be denied that this is a large order. Exactly because she is a participative religious she is exposed to the spirit of the world. More dangerously, she is threatened by its slow poisoning as drop by drop it threatens to seep into her mind and spiritual value estimation. Thus the very roots of spiritual living are endangered. Once this spiritual depth is gone she is no longer a witness for religion, though she may still wear the habit and the name. She is then merely a teacher, a social worker or whatever professional role she has in the world.

Because the participative religious is at the front of the spiritual struggle, she must take all the more care that her lived intimacy with God remains the center and core of her life. She has to take the necessary measures to safeguard her true spiritual dimension even though it may mean that she has to cut down on her professional duties. For every true religious this living with God must be the *highest* value. All the other aspects of her life come only in second place and they must cede whenever they are incompatible with her spiritual calling.

A priest I once knew was in charge of public relations. This meant in his case that he had to find the money necessary for the community and its works. He was practically always on the road. Though he was supposed to be in the monastery on Saturdays and Sundays, even then he was often absent. When he had done this work for a number of years, he started to realize that he was losing his spiritual depth. He tried hard to maintain his personal contact with God but he felt himself slipping more and more. He went to his superior and asked to be relieved of his job as otherwise he foresaw that it would lead to his downfall. The superior was a good man but he had no one else who could do the work as well. The money was badly needed and his request was refused. The priest struggled on but ended by leaving and getting married so that the community had to do without his services anyhow. Who was responsible? I don't know and it is not for me to judge. Nevertheless, if that priest had been given a chance to take care of his spiritual life, a valuable priest and religious might have been saved. Basically he was a good man but this kind of life simply was too much for him.

I give this story only as an example. Not all come to this extreme. Nevertheless, we all are in danger of getting so involved that our job takes over. What should be in second place takes the central stage and what should be the center becomes a secondary value only. Our spiritual life then loses its depth. We are uneasy, belonging neither to the world nor truly to God. We live in continuous conflict. It is sure that religious who are no longer anchored in God are not the inspirational witnesses they are called to be. As they themselves have lost the focus on their spiritual calling they cannot give to the world a loud and clear message that intimacy with God is meant to be the center of life for all men.

THE ROCKY ROAD

ON the day of our profession we all intended to take religious life seriously and to make God the main concern of our existence. Our whole novitiate had prepared us for such a firm resolution.

I still remember my novitiate. Our master of novices was a good man but he did not wear velvet gloves. From the very beginning he told us that he had never asked us to come and that he would never ask us to stay. If we wanted to stay it had to be our own decision. We had to observe the rules and do our best with the grace of God to change ourselves from world-oriented young men to God-oriented persons. He promised that he would eliminate whatever might hinder this process and if any one of us would become such an obstacle he would immediately remove this person. No, we were not pampered.

We started with the full program. Outside the two recreations a day there was strict silence. We had some manual labor, some classes of scripture and of the spiritual life and a daily conference. Besides the hours of meditation and spiritual reading, the day was interspersed with periods of free time. It was soon made clear to us that this free time could not be spent at will. It was called free time because we were then made free to pray and meditate. Coming straight from the world as lively young men, it was quite difficult to pray and meditate so much every day. The master of novices did his best to introduce us in this practice of prayer and meditation, but it took time before we could successfully attempt it. As the days became weeks and the weeks turned to months we discovered that we could be with God during the day. We learned to be with Him in the depth of our being and to live close to Him during our occupations. Doing this for a whole year under capable guidance we knew that we were no longer strangers in the spiritual life.

Though the master of novices at times expressed doubt that we would ever be good religious, we realized that we could not be too bad when we were allowed to make our profession. We knew what we were in for. The master had reminded us many times about the hardships we would have to face, the sometimes difficult confreres, the occasionally unreasonable superiors. So what? It would not be always easy but every form of life has its difficulties. Moreover, we knew we were not alone. If God would send us these troubles, He would also give the strength to meet them.

As a result, when we made our profession, we were happy to totally dedicate ourselves to God. We had a reasonable certitude that with His grace we could and would become good religious. As a matter of fact we were rather sure that we would be better religious than many of the fathers who after years of religious life were in our view far from perfect men. This attitude on our part was unadulterated pride but we were still so young and inexperienced in the ways of spiritual life. After our profession we were ready to go.

Looking now at myself after all these years and at my confreres of the novitiate, it is clear that as a whole we have turned out to be just the same as the fathers upon whom we looked down at the end of the novitiate. None of us has become the perfect man we intended to be. We still have our faults, our temper, our irritation and envy. Some have made a career in the academic field, others worked as missionaries, others again as pastors in parishes but none has become the faultless religious we were all planning to become.

Are we bad people? Not at all. Are we bad religious? In no way. What then was wrong? Something must have been wrong if none of us reached the ideal of the perfect religious we intended to be. We were wrong in believing that we had the power to eliminate all our faults. We imagined that in our continuing progress no defect could survive. It is true that our master of novices had warned us that we would have to struggle with our deficiencies and that we would be imperfect till the end of our days but we did not really believe that. *We* were sincere! We were *totally* dedicated to God! Though we still had some faults it would be only a question of time before we had eliminated the last one of them. How naive we were!

Our mistake was that we thought that it was enough to will a thing to make it come about. This view not only disregards God's plan with our lives but it also overlooks the factual reality that I am not just a will but also body, emotions, and all these faculties and drives which constitute the whole man.

As religious we have dedicated our whole selves to God in a free surrender of love and we have chosen Him as the center of our lives. This dedication is only possible insofar as I will it with the grace of God. We may surmise that at our profession we sincerely and resolutely willed this total dedication. But this is not the whole story. This intimacy with the divine has to radiate into the rest of our being so that our thoughts, words and deeds are taken up in this divine orientation and become means as well as manifestations of this deep inner life. It is here that we meet many difficulties.

Perhaps it has happened to you that you were to meet a person whom you disliked very much. You were aware of that aversion and wanted to behave as a good Christian should. You decided that in spite of everything this was going to be a nice interview. She comes in and you greet her kindly. You listen to her with all the kindness you have. But suddenly, perhaps because of what she says or because of the way she looks at you all your mildness is gone. What started as a quiet conversation ends in a shouting match of two angry persons telling each other off.

Such events show that we do not have an absolute control over all the facets of our selves. I can at will move my hand left or right or not move it at all. But my emotion, my temper, my anxiety and fear all too easily escape my control and go on a rampage which I do not really want or approve but which just seems to carry me away.

Before our novitiate we were subject to these faults but during the novitiate we learned with the grace of God to improve ourselves. We naively believed that, though we were not perfect, the end of the struggle was in sight. Once returned to the life of work or study, we discovered to our dismay that we had the same faults as before and perhaps even some new ones. How can we explain this?

During our novitiate spiritual living was the central and exclusive focusing point. The rule, the exercises and the whole atmosphere were conducive to that. The attempt of spiritual living brought with it an effort to improve our daily faults. Due to this concentration on the spiritual and aided by the grace of God the young novice was able to check these deficiencies at least to some degree. This success led her to believe that she had all but overcome these wrong tendencies. Unfortunately, in most cases she merely learned to prevent the actualization of these faults while the roots were still deeply present in her.

The Ven. Libermann writes that these imperfections are like weeds. In order to eliminate them the gardener has to rake and clear the soil. But the weeds are not gone yet. Soon they show themselves again and the weeding has to start anew. Only after long and repeated raking is there a possibility that the roots will die off and the weeds be gone for good. The novice is careful that the weeds of her faults don't manifest themselves. At the smallest sign that they are growing up again she takes appropriate action to prevent further spreading. Doing this regularly she may reach a moment when the soil of her life does not show any weeds but she thinks too easily that the roots have also disappeared. All those experienced in the spiritual life know that the dying of these roots may take a lifetime while some of them may never disappear totally.

On leaving the novitiate the religious is placed in work or study. She now has to take care of many things besides her spiritual progress. New demands are made which may come in the form of extra work, a paper to be finished, an exam to be prepared. She is in new surroundings with new companions and social activities. No wonder the young religious is confused in the beginning. She needs a qualified director who can guide her through this period of adjustment. Because her attention is absorbed by the multiplicity of things, the watchfulness over her daily faults diminishes and they show themselves again. At the same time she experiences difficulties in remaining united with God during the day. She easily becomes discouraged. She does not realize that her present condition simply shows how weak she still is in the spiritual life. She may conclude that she has lost everything she had acquired during the novitiate.

A good director will make clear that this is not the case. During the novitiate, when her whole life was centered on living with God, she learned to overcome the obstacles that were present. Now in her new situation as student or professional worker she faces other obstacles which in turn she must learn to handle with the grace of God and use as a means to grow in depth. The spark of divine life that was enkindled during the novitiate must now be made to radiate in her thoughts, words and deeds. But this takes time. It is a process of growth that lasts till the end of her days. Some of the difficulties she will be able to overcome, while others will haunt her as long as she lives. She must learn to realize that in some of her faults success will never be hers but that as long as she keeps trying to improve herself she shows and lives her love for God.

A confrere of mine had a very bad temper at the

time I made his acquaintance. Any little adversity could make him explode and it was rather difficult to live with him in the same community. About thirty years later he died and though his temper was not as easily roused as in his younger days it still provided a daily abundance of explosions. He was still a difficult man to live with. All admitted that he was a good man but that temper ... He certainly was not considered a holy man. Nevertheless, those who knew him more intimately had quite a different opinion. This man did not make himself. He was born with a difficult temper and he was the first one to wish that it were not so. There would not have been much of a problem if his temper were always under perfect control of his will. But anyone who has the same handicap knows that it does not work that way. Before we are aware of it, before our will has any grip on the situation, we are already carried away on the flood of our fury. It is true that other people suffered from this man's lack of control but no one suffered as much as he himself. He was basically a well intentioned man, wanting to be patient and understanding, but it was all to no avail once any contrariety inflamed him.

He was also an intelligent man who had a clear understanding of his own condition. He saw very well that unless something extraordinary happened he would die still subject to these furies. But he succeeded in turning this personal handicap into an advantage on the spiritual level. He did not become depressed about his uncontrollable fits of temper. Though he felt bad about them, they never got him down. He saw his difficulty as a permanent challenge, as an invitation from above to show his love for God precisely in this area. Thus day after day, month after month and year after year, every morning anew he made the firm resolve to do what he could to control his temper that day. Why? Because he loved God. He felt that God had given him this temper so that in all humility he could show his love for God in this daily attempt at improvement, all the while knowing that he would never really make it. What a perseverance he showed, what a dedication, what a love that never gave up in this evidently hopeless and unsuccessful struggle. But was it really unsuccessful? It would have been if he had set as his goal to perfectly control his temper. He was too realistic and too spiritual for that. His only goal was to show God his ardent love in *trying* to improve his temper and here he was, with God's grace, enormously successful. It was this weakness that daily made him cling closer to God. It was this lack of external success that burned away his pride and self-centeredness. This daily attempt out of love for God effected a deep union with the divine in the depth of his being, where the true essence of holiness exists. It was the trying that counted, that always renewed, never slacking, firm but peaceful attempt, not in order to show success (though he would have loved it for himself as well as for others) but as a total unselfish surrender in love, an answer to the divine love for him. He certainly was not a pleasant confrere to live with if one looked merely at the external side of his daily behavior. But those who knew him more intimately could not but be impressed with the deep spirituality and the lived union with God that radiated in his daily life.

The essence of true holiness resides in that deep spiritual center of our being where with the fullness of our will we surrender in love to God. Because of this love we attempt to make our dedication radiate in the totality of our being, in our thoughts, words and actions so that these too are taken up in this deeper orientation to God. The fact that we attempt this spiritualization of our whole being does not guarantee that we shall succeed. This success depends not only on the grace of God but also on the factual make-up of our whole self with its drives, desires and emotions.

A person who has a phlegmatic constitution will not be subject to frequent outbursts of temper. It would be absurd to think that because of this even disposition she is holier than one who has a bad temper. Having no fits of temper may be simply due to her make-up and not a particular manifestation of her love for God. It is quite possible that her difficulty is the opposite of that found in a hot-tempered person. Her apathy may incline her to avoid necessary energetic action so that this very inclination is an imperfection she must try to overcome. Such a person may be more pleasant to live with but this does not mean that she is more intimately united with God than someone who, out of love for God, daily attempts to master her uncontrollable temper.

We can all point to aspects in our lives which in spite of our sincere efforts refuse to be taken up in our interior orientation and thus to become spiritualized. Unfortunately, in facing these faults many mistakes are made, though often with the best of intentions.

Notice that when we speak about faults we do not mean serious faults. We speak here about dedicated religious who by their vocation itself and by the grace of God avoid all serious moral offenses. The faults we mention are those imperfections to which we are all subject even though we earnestly strive to live a deep spiritual life.

It would be a wrong attitude to discard these faults with the saying: "I cannot worry about little things." Though it does no good to *worry* about little things we must not neglect to pay attention to them. When we made our profession we surrendered our whole selves out of love for God. We were resolved to bring all aspects of our lives into our spiritual orientation as far as, with the grace of God, this would be possible. Refusing to continue this attempt at spiritual integration is taking back at least partially what we have promised. Anyone who implicitly or explicitly takes this attitude should seriously examine her love for God. True love tries to please the Beloved in all and the more intense this love the more we experience the indelicacy of even a small neglect. Maybe we have lost this refined sense of love and have opened the path that leads down. This is not a purely imaginary possibility. Refusal to pay attention to our small faults means failure to keep them in check. We unlearn the ability to handle them properly and do not realize how they increase their power over us. In the spiritual life one does not at once fall from high to low. It is the gradual decline that brings about our inability to stop when the abyss opens up.

It is also a wrong attitude when we want to improve ourselves merely because our faults make us look bad or diminish our chances for promotion or success. Though these considerations certainly have their value, if our motivation does not reach beyond them, we act totally outside the spiritual realm.

Neither is it enough to reject these faults merely because they hurt somebody else. This again is a valid consideration but if this is our sole foundation we are mere humanists and again have not reached the spiritual level.

Because the spiritually dedicated person loves God she desires to make her whole existence a hymn to God's glory, an offering of praise, gratitude and love. All her words, thoughts and actions she wishes to be an incarnation of the divine love as it lives in her. The more she experiences the greatness and goodness of God, the more she sees her faults as a falling short in her answer to His love. For some this awareness becomes a source of anxiety. They sincerely do their best. But if they really did their best should they not be able to overcome these faults? Hence they conclude that they do not really do their best. They must intensify their attempts but in doing so they become more and more tense. The unfortunate result is that not only do they not eliminate these faults but in their tension and anxiety they commit new ones. This opens the way to the temptation to give up their effort to improve as an impossible dream.

These good persons do not realize that they have set their own goal in the spiritual life. *They* are going to do it. They are inspired by a pious intention. Because God is the all-good, the all-perfect, nothing but the best is good enough for Him. Only a life without any fault seems worthy of the divine love. Unfortunately they forget that true holiness does not require actual perfect external behavior but the *sincere attempt* to make intimacy with God direct one's whole life to Him. The success of this effort depends not only upon our physical and psychological make-up but also, and above all, upon God's grace. The history of spirituality makes clear that even in the saints God allows some faults to persist until death. Only the Blessed Virgin is an exception.

Why would God allow such an unsuccessful struggle? Calling this struggle unsuccessful shows that we have not yet grasped its true value for spiritual life. The basis of all spirituality is the intensity and the intimacy of our union with God in the depth of our being. Growing in holiness, in love of God, means increasing this intensity of intimate union. *That* is holiness and that is what we should strive for. In this we shall never fail if we are faithful to God's grace.

On the other hand, we must always remember that in the supernatural order we can do nothing of ourselves. Only the grace of God can make us work effectively and thus we can never go beyond the grace God gives us. Trying to do so is reaching beyond that to which we are called. We are then left without God's sustaining and fortifying grace and are bound to fail.

This striving to a growing intimacy with the divine is connected with but distinguished from our ability to bring the rest of our being, our words, thoughts and actions within this spiritual orientation. When we really love God we shall try to sanctify and perfect our whole being. Failing to do so is failing in love. Because this sanctification of our words, thoughts and actions can come about only by grace, here too we cannot go further than this grace allows us to go. It is the trying that counts and not the success. Deep spiritual life is possible without total *actual* orientation to God of the rest of our being. Normally, when we take spiritual life seriously God grants us the grace to make progress in this spiritualization but there are always some aspects which resist our honest effort of improvement.

The struggle to correct these faults is not unsuccessful in relation to growing intimacy with God. The very attempt, inspired by love, brings us closer to Him. This struggle can be called unsuccessful only insofar as the actual faults are not definitely overcome. Why would God allow their continuance?

It is impossible for man to gauge the depth of God's wisdom and free action but a closer consideration of the human condition gives us some insight. One of the greatest obstacles to spiritual life is human pride which is attributing to oneself that which finds its source in God. Anyone who has attempted to deepen intimacy with God or who has studied those who apply themselves to it knows that this pride is always standing in the wings ready to take the bows to which it has no rights. The more one advances in spiritual depth the more subtle and dangerous become the disguises of human pride. An antidote is found in the rather rude awakening which our weakness and our faults provide. They make us vividly aware that only through God's grace can we live united with Him.

What would happen if one succeeded in overcoming all his faults? It would mean that we no longer experience acutely our weakness and sinfulness which are always present as a potential danger as well as a reminder of our need of God's assistance. Seeing the human condition as it is, it seems doubtful that we could avoid the arrogance of attributing the success to ourselves. Our pride would all too easily take the credit where ultimately it is God who brought us that far. God in His goodness could keep us in His intimacy and overcome this pride but a realistic look at ourselves makes clear that we shall always need some antidote to bring our existence in the proper balance. If our imperfections would all be overcome something else would have to be given to keep alive the awareness that only God can redeem and save us.

In this light we can understand why even in great saints God allows these imperfections to continue. They constitute a painful but healthy reminder that man can never save himself and that the work of salvation depends on grace.

Considered in an abstract way it is not so difficult to accept this truth. Quite different is the question when I want to know why *I have to keep struggling with these specific imperfections.* Very often there is only one possible answer: "I don't know." It sometimes happens that in looking back over my life I can understand why at a certain moment this or that happened to me. Usually at the moment itself of the happening I have no other insight than *that* it must be meaningful and good for me though I do not see or understand why. Analyzing the frustration this ignorance evokes I realize that it comes forth from the desire to know clearly where I am going and what God is doing with me. I have the illusion that if I knew what the divine plan with my life was, I would have greater trust in His goodness and wisdom. But just the opposite takes place. Trust is practiced only when I do *not* see where the other is leading me. To the degree that I myself demand insight and want the other to give an account of what he is doing, to that degree I have lost my trust in him. Instead of chafing against this ignorance I must see it as an invitation to greater trust in the divine wisdom and love.

I treat God as God only insofar as I give Him unlimited credit concerning my life and allow Him a free hand concerning my future. Demanding insight when this is not given is desiring to take over control instead of a limitless trust in His goodness. If I really want to grow spiritually through my persistent imperfections, of which I do not see the reason, I must all the more completely surrender to Him. "You want me to struggle. As you love me infinitely, it must be good for me. I thank you and accept wholeheartedly."

From what we have said it is evident that we should never give up this trying to improve our faults, though we may foresee that we shall never master at least some of them. This trying is important not only because it prevents us from further slipping back but also because it is a constant actualization of our love for God. The surrender to God is not a once and for all operation but a lifelong process. These apparently invincible faults become repeated invitations to exercise factually this love in the attempt to counteract and overcome them. This love is all the more pure because no other satisfaction comes to us than the satisfaction to have done the best we could precisely because we love God. Though this effort may never lead to the success of overcoming these imperfections it is, nevertheless, a continuous manifestation and deepening of our love for God. It opens the way to a greater intimacy with Him and greater holiness.

Once we realize that these imperfections do not prevent our spiritual growth but are the occasions of greater deepening, we shall be more able to overcome any anxiety they provoke. The saints emphasize that God allows these imperfections in order to give us a deeper awareness of our weakness and His goodness. Instead of becoming depressed by our faults we must use them as an occasion to foster greater love and surrender. Precisely because these difficulties show us how weak we are, they urge us to cling to God with greater fidelity. They make us more aware of the constant need of redemption and help us to face Him more sincerely as our Redeemer. The great secret of spiritual living is to turn whatever may become an obstacle into occasions of greater love for God and thus to greater holiness.

The permanence of these imperfections should never be an occasion for discouragement. When we become discouraged it means that we have set for ourselves a standard of perfection beyond that which God's grace wants us now to reach. All spiritual authors insist that we should follow the grace of God and never be ahead of it because we then no longer walk God's path and have become side-tracked. The truly religious person does not get upset by his daily imperfections, which he has firmly tried to overcome so far without success. In all humility he places everything in God's hands knowing that what He wants is for man's good. His life then becomes peaceful. He is happy because God is with him even though he has faults. He still feels sorry that he fails but he watches that this remorse does not disturb his inner harmony. He is aware that any movement that threatens this peace cannot come from God.

Such a person will not be spared the miseries and sorrows of life and he does not want to be spared. He accepts the fact that following Christ is sharing with Him the way to Calvary. Though darkness may invade his soul and suffering his body, in the inner depth there is peace and joy. United with God in love he accepts as good whatever happens. Though he is imperfect, he sees this as good too insofar as it is a lasting occasion for greater love and an invitation to get closer to God.

APPROACHING THE LIGHT

THE focus of any good novitiate is the spiritual transformation of the novices. The structure of the program, the horarium, the classes, the work, all have one goal: to bring the young person to a personal contact with God in the center of her being. Unless she comes to this initial intimacy with the divine she should not be allowed to make her profession.

This does not mean that one cannot come to deep spiritual living without a novitiate. When I was young, my dad had his own vegetable garden. Every spring he sowed various seeds on wooden shelves covered with earth. I still remember how I observed the little stems piercing the surface and growing tiny leaves. When they were big enough dad took them to his garden and planted them at the required distance from one another so that they could grow into full plants. Why did he not sow the seed directly in his garden? Because indoors the temperature was quite constant and the seeds could be watered in time, they had a much better chance of starting a healthy growth. When they were planted outside they had already grown strong enough to withstand the sometimes unfavorable climatic conditions.

The sole purpose of the novitiate is to allow the

novice to grow spiritual roots. One who has no novitiate can also become a spiritual person but she will be in a less favorable condition than the novice whose life for at least one whole year is centered around intimacy with God.

When the novice makes her profession, her formation is not yet finished. She learned to live with God in daily life amidst the favorable surroundings of the novitiate. The young religious was privileged to be initiated in an atmosphere of prayer, silence and recollection. She now has to make her re-entry into the world of work in such a way that what she has acquired during the novitiate is not lost but starts effectively radiating in her personal life and work.

This is an especially critical period in the life of each religious. The protective surroundings of the novitiate have fallen away. Her life at once is so crowded with interests of study and work that she becomes confused. It is the task of the director to teach the young religious how the life of work and study can be harmoniously taken up in the attempt of continuous spiritualization. Only through this constant spiritual deepening can she be a true witness in her life and work of the possibility, the beauty and the joy of living with God. Without this growing spiritual depth she may be a good teacher or nurse or whatever profession she chooses, but as a *religious* she has failed.

At our profession we were resolved to maintain our

personal contact with God. The practice of life showed us very soon that true spiritual life can be maintained only at the cost of an always renewed effort. Though we are of good will and love God sincerely, it is nevertheless difficult to sustain our spiritual impetus.

During the novitiate there were relatively few factors which averted our attention from focusing on God. Even when such an event did happen, we soon returned to our main interest, living with God. After profession it was a different situation. Study and work as well as new surroundings started to crowd our imagination and emotions. If we were sent to study we had to worry about papers, exams and grades. We also took part in social activities. All these occupations deeply involved us. We sincerely attempted to live our spiritual life but since so much of our time was filled with other interests we had to take care of prayer and meditation in periods between these activities. Soon we discovered that our work or study invaded also these in-between moments. During meditation we caught ourselves developing a term paper. At Mass we were trying to find a solution for a difficult math problem. Try as we might we just could not keep our minds on Christ or on whatever was the topic of our prayer. Sometimes we tried forcefully to keep our mind and imagination under control but had to give that up when it resulted in a headache.

The young religious in such a situation is still fully dedicated to God but in the practical life other concerns take over more and more. Temptation then starts its whisper. "Why should I keep trying to pray and meditate if it does not work at all?" From there it is only one step to the neglect of spiritual life. "I just cannot do everything. First things first. I have three exams plus two term papers and these *must* be finished in time."

The basic weakness and mistake of the young religious is that she starts living a schizoid existence. She tries to take care of God *and* her work instead of attempting to find God *in* her work. The union and living with God is not a part-time affair. It is a fundamental attitude that pervades our whole lives, our words and actions. Only with this attitude can we develop a harmonious spiritual life. How do we acquire such an attitude?

Although we all live in the same world, this world does not have the same meaning for everyone. When a group of people visit a lake, one may say: "What an occasion for a swim." Another: "What a fishing spot." The artistic person will be touched by its beauty while the ecologist worries about its pollution. The same reality of the lake will have a different meaning according to each one's interest. Though all see the same reality, everyone discovers a meaning that corresponds to her background, culture and formation. The more central a specific interest is, the more a person will discover in reality facets that correspond to this dominating factor. For one whose main interest is sex a church tower will be a sexual symbol. For the artist it will be a work of beauty and for the spiritual person it will be a finger pointing to God. The meaning the world of reality has for us, the meaning we discover there spontaneously is in correspondence with our personal interests and especially with our central value. The world will have a spiritual meaning for me, will manifest God to me, to the degree that my central interest is the Divine and His love.

The young religious who experiences that worldly things crowd her mind and interest should not be discouraged. Because she is just a beginner, her spiritual orientation is not yet so anchored that she will discover everywhere the divine love. All she can do and has to do is to start every day anew to deepen this central dimension of her life so that with God's grace it becomes the dominating value.

The question then comes: How can I maintain and deepen this spiritual orientation in order to allow it to permeate not only my personal life but also my work?

Through our profession we have made lived union with God the central core of our existence. This intimacy can never be reached nor increased unless I regularly approach God in a personal encounter. For this reason all spiritual masters of all times agree that no healthy spiritual life is possible without regular meditation. Under the old rule this was at least exteriorly taken care of. Every morning we got up, went to the chapel, said morning prayers and tried to meditate. It was the same rule for all, notwithstanding the fact that at this early morning hour some were not in the best physical and psychological condition for meditation. In many communities the renewal has changed this so that each individual can choose the hour of meditatation that suits her best.

But new troubles arose. Some interpreted the new rule to mean that they should make their meditation at the time they feel like it. Soon they discovered that rather seldom do they feel like it. Waiting for this mood means that days and even weeks pass by without any meditation at all. The more irregular they are at meditation the more difficult it becomes; the danger is great that they give it up altogether. Needless to say that this causes serious harm to their spiritual life.

Others are convinced of the need for daily meditation and decide that they will use the first quiet moments the day provides. Unfortunately, too many days pass by without any quiet moments and, therefore, without meditation.

We must realize that where outside rules have fallen away, we must all the more strongly cultivate a personal rule to which we hold as much as possible.

We must establish a fixed time for our meditation. It may be in the morning or in the evening or at any time that suits us. But then we must hold on to it and consider our meditation as the really important thing we have to do at that moment. There can, of course, be serious reasons which oblige us to postpone this encounter with God but if these reasons occur too many times we have to choose another moment less subject to intrusions.

There is still another factor to be considered. Suppose that every day, right after my classes, I have sufficient time to make my meditation. There is a good possibility that during this period I continue to settle my school problems. I am still so keyed up about my work that it is difficult to be quietly with God. If it is the only time available, I have to make the best of it but it certainly would be preferable if I could find an hour during which I could enter my mental prayer without already being encumbered and occupied with various problems and difficulties. For this reason the old masters of spirituality preferred the early morning hours. The day is then still fresh and relatively uncluttered. Some will object that at that hour they themselves are not fresh at all. Everyone has to decide for herself, unless the rule prescribes a fixed hour. When the choice is left to us, all we have to do is to choose the moment that is best for us. We then show our good will and love for God.

In mental prayer we meet God in solitude. This

solitude is above all an inner attitude. We remove from our attention all creatures, not in order to forget them but to find them in their deepest center which is God. We look at them with the eyes of God so that they do not become an obstacle to our union with Him but an incentive.

To come to this inner solitude, the place where we make our meditation is helpful. We must choose a place that as far as possible does not present us with new distractions of which we certainly have enough already. For some this place will be their room, for others the chapel, a quiet corridor or a path in the garden. Once you have found such a place, remain with it. The more you get used to it the less it will open new areas for distraction.

During meditation you may quietly kneel or sit. The more nervous types prefer to walk while others combine the two ways. Whatever you choose is unimportant as long as it helps you to be united with God.

A ticklish point is our preparation for meditation. It may sound strange to insist on it. Nobody who is going to meet her mother feels the need to prepare her conversation beforehand. If our contact with God were of the same nature as that with our mother there would be no difficulty. Once another human being is present we perceive her with our senses and, when we are acquainted with the person, a conversation easily follows, though not always on a personal level. God is beyond our senses. To come into personal contact with Him through His grace we have to go deeper into ourselves. There we are opened to His presence. This inner openness is something we have to acquire and it rarely comes easily. We therefore have to look for means that will guide us to God. We must prepare our meditation so that we have at hand thoughts, truths and perspectives which can help us to reach out to Him. If His grace during meditation guides us by a different route, all we have to do is to follow this guidance and forget what we have prepared. But this does not happen too often.

Anyone who regularly approaches mental prayer without proper preparation knows that her meditation falls flat. She will try one topic after another but they all come to a dead end and when the time is passed she has not yet truly begun to meditate.

It would be a fallacy to think that everything will go smoothly when we choose the right time and the right place and prepare our topic. Anyone who is faithful to her daily meditation knows better. Meditation is a valuable means of deepening our spiritual life but this spiritual life is in the very center of our being. There, in what the spiritual authors call the fine point of the soul, we have to grow intimately united with God as a person. In our meditation we have to go beyond senses and imagination. We have to learn to leave the sensible and imaginary world behind and in the depth of ourselves reach for the divine with our intellect and will.

For most people who start the spiritual life this is an unknown way of being present. Only one who has reached this openness can truly understand what it means. For those who are starting out it is a groping without precisely knowing for what. For this reason spiritual authors have worked out various methods which are all good under the condition that they suit the user. These methods serve the same function as parallel bars for one who after an operation has to learn again to walk. Without them she does not go anywhere, but once she has learned to walk again she no longer uses them. Nevertheless, on a small mountain path we are glad to find a railing to hold onto in case we get dizzy. The beginner in the spiritual life uses the method but only as a means to come to this inner personal contact with God. Once she has learned how to reach this she discards the method insofar as it is no longer useful. She follows then the guidance of the Spirit. But when at times the Spirit is silent return to the method may be helpful.

The beginner uses her imagination quite regularly. She imagines, for example, Christ suffering in the Garden of Olives. She must, however, remember that it is not enough to look merely at this imaginary picture. As long as she limits herself to the consideration of this product of her imagination she has not yet reached Christ Himself as a person. The consideration of the agony in the garden, as she imagines it, must merely be a guide to meeting Christ in a person to person encounter. Once she arrives at this personal presence to Christ she must stay with it, as long as it lasts, in love, surrender or whatever pious actions are brought about. In the beginning these moments of truly being with God are short. But if one is faithful to her meditation and really puts her heart in it, she will discover it becomes rather easy to place oneself from the beginning of meditation in this personal contact with the divine and to remain there as long as God gives this grace to her.

At this stage of progress there comes a difficulty which always plagues us in mental prayer but is now more bothersome. It is the difficulty of distractions. This difficulty is easy to understand but hard to handle. Although we may improve as time goes on we shall never be able to overcome it totally.

Once we have acquired a certain ease in being personally present to God in our meditation, we face Him in loving attention and surrender. We simply *love* Him. Loving, however, is an activity of the will by which we place ourselves totally at His disposal. At that moment our imagination and analytic mind are without their specific object and function. Over these faculties we have no absolute control. We may wish them to be quiet but they are not. While in dedicated presence we are facing God these faculties keep busy

and drag from our consciousness and subconscious-
ness all kinds of images and concepts.

A first reaction is to try to suppress their activity
forcefully but this is never successful for long.
Keeping up this forceful pressure makes all mental
prayer impossible as it leads us away from the real
goal and center of our meditation which is God. We
become so busy with our unruly thoughts and images
that we have no attention left to be with Him. This
does not mean that we should give in to these
distractions because then too we would lose presence
to God.

How then to handle these disturbing distractions?
The only sensible approach is to let them be. It may
happen to you that while you are studying in your
room a horsefly makes its entry. You do not see it
but its buzzing makes its presence unmistakably
known. You try to catch it but after several vain
attempts you have to give up. You can now do two
things. You may get irritated and follow its every
move so that you don't study at all or you may
consider it as just one of those unpleasant things and
continue your study.

Our distractions are like that fly. They buzz and
are annoying but as long as you don't allow yourself
to be taken in by them you can continue your
peaceful presence to God. This does not mean that
you will always succeed. You will catch yourself

occupied with these phantasies and thoughts. Don't get angry or discouraged. This simply is the human condition. Learn to smile at yourself and without tension but gently and peacefully place yourself again in God's presence. The stronger our union with God becomes the better we learn to handle this difficulty without, however, totally mastering it.

This is not the end of our woes. All of us have experienced that once we have entered our meditation and try to be present to God He does not seem to be there. We are like one crying in the desert. God does not answer. Trying to go back to a former stage by, for example, using our imagination as an inductive factor does not work either. One way to keep ourselves occupied, then, is to start thinking. If we succeed in elaborating a whole series of clever and pious ideas, we may think that we have made a good meditation. Incorrectly so. The goal of meditation is not to exercise our mind in reasoning and elaborating brilliant ideas but to become closer united to God. While we were intellectually figuring things out, we were only occupied with concepts but the person of God as person did not enter anywhere.

Some think that the answer is to read a spiritual book. Such a book may be of great value insofar as it can help us to place ourselves in God's presence. Because in this period of spiritual aridity God does not seem to be present, we may be inclined to keep on reading. Again we have been constantly occupied but we have not been present to God nor deepened our union with Him.

What then should we do when, after placing ourselves in God's presence as well as we could, there is only a dark silent cloud? All we have to do is to remain quietly waiting for God in peaceful loving attention and surrender. Whenever we discover that we have drifted away we must gently bring our attention back to Him.

Especially in the beginning it demands courage and perseverance to be faithful to our mental prayer when day after day and week after week there is nothing but darkness and silence. The temptation to give up may become very strong. "What is the use of it all? It is understandable that one knocks again on a door when the first knock brings no result. But it seems pretty senseless to keep knocking when even after repeated attempts there is no answer. Either there is nobody home or whoever is home does not want to see me."

Christ Himself gave the answer to this difficulty. "Suppose one of you has a friend and goes to him in the middle of the night to say, 'My friend, lend me three loaves because a friend of mind on his travels has just arrived at my house and I have nothing to offer him'; and the man answers from inside the house, 'Do not bother me. The door is bolted now, and my children are in bed; I cannot get up to give it to you.' I tell you, if the man does not get up and give it to him for friendship's sake, persistence will be enough to make him get up and give his friend all he wants.

So I say to you: ask, and it will be given to you; search, and you will find; knock and the door will be opened to you. For the one who asks always receives; the one who searches always finds; the one who knocks will always have the door opened to him. What father among you would hand his son a stone when he asked for bread? Or hand him a snake instead of a fish? Or hand him a scorpion if he asked for an egg? If you then, who are evil, know how to give your children what is good, how much more will the heavenly Father give the Holy Spirit to those who ask Him!" Lk. 11, 5-13.

The moral is clear. Keep knocking! God is there, concerned with us even though He seems far away. In His own good time He will make us experience His presence again. We don't know when this will be but don't give up!

These periods of aridity are an occasion as well as an invitation to deepen our faith. Faith means opening to God an unlimited credit, an absolute trust without any questions asked. When in our meditation we are dry as a cactus in the desert, let us not waste our time by trying to find out why God treats us *now* this way. Simply and peacefully convey to Him that you accept whatever He wants, that you have an absolute trust in His goodness and are willing to wait even if this means waiting till death.

But there is more. The living of religion means living with God in a person to person relationship of loving surrender. "Loving surrender." We formulate these words so easily, but they are meaningful only when in our lives we attempt to realize the program they express. To surrender means to hand over one's right to the other, let him decide. A surrender to God, then, is to place our lives in His hands, to follow His call and invitation, to make His plans ours. The religious has made this surrender the center of her life. It is a total surrender whereby she places herself at the disposal of God's loving care. This surrender is given not because we *have to do it* but as a loving answer to His infinite love which went so far that He gave His life for us.

When we made our profession we were sincerely resolved to practice this total surrender in our daily lives. But making this resolution is a long way removed from its actual day by day realization. We are still full of self-centeredness, selfishness, pride and self-importance. In this light we can somewhat understand the great value of the periods of aridity which we have to go through in our spiritual ascent. When in meditation we try to reach out and find only darkness, there is nothing here that is pleasing to our natural human faculties. Why then do we go on? Because we *love* Him. This love can sustain us only

[98]

when we allow it to be purified from all return to self, when it becomes a love that is totally focused on God because He is *lovable*. It is this love, cleansed more and more from our selfishness, that gives us the patience to wait in darkness, as long as He wants us to wait, even, if He desires so, till the end of our days. This loving selfless surrender has only one goal: to please Him, to manifest to Him that we are totally dedicated to His love.

No one has truly learned to love God and to surrender to Him totally unless he has gone through this tunnel of darkness where slowly but steadily are burned away the obstacles to the coming of the Holy Spirit. This path is certainly a path of suffering but it is a sweet suffering in love and for love, enlightened by the awareness in faith that we really follow Christ and share in the redemption of mankind. Paradox-ically, in totally giving himself to God, man becomes a truly human person, more harmonious in the depth of his being. His unique path is manifested more clearly and he can now work with greater ease at the self-realization to which God has called him.

In mental prayer there is never a reason to be discouraged. As long as during my daily meditation I try to remain in God's presence in a peaceful surrender of love I make a good meditation. I may not feel anything, I may not see my progress, but this is not important. The important thing is to faithfully show God my love and surrender purely because He is who He is, the infinite Love. In true mental prayer it is God who counts and not I. However, because I thus empty myself from myself, He will more and more dominate that center of my being through His Spirit and intensify His living within me. This growth will be mostly unnoticed.

A mother who has her children around her daily will not every day be aware of their growth. She will see it, nevertheless, when Jimmy's pants get too short and Mary's coat too small. In a similar way our daily increase in spiritual depth escapes our attention but at certain moments we are aware that we have changed, that we have more ease of being with God during the day, that we more spontaneously discover God's love behind the vicissitudes of life. As long as we are honestly and peacefully faithful there is no reason to worry.

Even when we have been unfaithful, when under the pressure of work, tension or other circumstances we have neglected our spiritual life, even then there is no reason to be discouraged. Though we may run away from God, He is always waiting, ready to receive us when we come back. As with our other faults we should use this infidelity as a lever to direct us more honestly to God. We have now experienced that we are weak and shall never make it on our own. This must incite us to cling more closely to Him in a peaceful but firm determination. Staying in the dumps is no good. Start again and be generous! God will always be more generous.

There are during the day still other occasions which aid us in deepening our union with God.

First of all there is assistance at Mass. In this supreme act Christ renews the sacrifice of Himself to the Father in full obedience. Those who partake in this liturgy join by offering themselves with Christ. Through the sacred meal they become united with Christ in a special way and are strengthened by His grace. Partaking in the Holy Eucharist involves more than physically being present and joining in song and prayer. This partaking is above all a sharing in the attitude of Christ which is an attitude of total obedience. In loving surrender He gives Himself up to His Father's wishes without any reservation, not even that of His life. True assistance at Mass means uniting ourselves with Christ in this complete surrender. Our worship is authentic when together with Christ we give ourselves up to the Father's wishes without any reservation. In this way assistance at Mass is a renewed accentuation of the commitment we have made at our profession.

Before the renewal being present at Mass was a part of the daily routine. Some people object to obligatory attendence because, they say, it results in a careless fulfillment of this obligation. They make a fundamental mistake. If they carelessly assist at Mass, it is not because attendance is prescribed but because they are careless persons.

After the renewal some constitutions no longer state that the sisters have to attend daily Mass. If they do attend, it is because they want to. But unless the careless persons have changed their attitude they will discover that they still are present in a careless way. From there it is only one step to the question: "Why should I go to daily Mass when it means nothing to me?" The answer to this question is very simple, though probably not appealing to persons in this predicament. They say that the Mass means nothing to them. This, of course, must not be taken literally as it would indicate that they have lost their faith. Normally this is not so. What they mean is that the Mass does not make them feel anything. So what? The living of religion and the sharing in the sacraments is not a question of feeling but of personal dedication and loving surrender. When in the aridity of our spiritual life we sincerely join with Christ in surrendering ourselves to the Father, our surrender is all the more sincere. We give ourselves up to the Father's wishes purely out of love for Him and not because we obtain any immediate satisfaction.

Once we return to the lived conviction that this act is of tremendous value we shall again be aware of its profound meaning. This does not mean that we shall have no distractions and sometimes even boredom. But we must treat this the same way as distraction in mental prayer. Peacefully and gently we must bring ourselves back to sharing with Christ in His oblation.

"But do we have to go to daily Mass? So many good Christians assist at Mass only on Sundays. Why should we do more?" It is true, unfortunately, that some religious by their own choice assist at Mass only on Sunday. Though they may be of good intention, it is beyond doubt that their spiritual viewpoint is seriously out of focus. The religious by her own free will and decision has dedicated her life to God. She has chosen living with Him as the central concern of her life, not out of fear, neither by commercial contract (I give you so much if you give me that) but out of love. Love is the dominating and determining factor in the relationship between the religious and God.

When two persons truly love one another they do not ask how much *they have to do* but how much *they can do* to please the beloved and show their love. As soon as one starts calculating how much she has to do, she has left the realm of love and the relationship has become that of contractual obligation. True love certainly will observe these obligations but it goes further. The true measure of love is to have no measure. Love is the unselfish caring for the good of the other. In this view, which is the only appropriate view of religious life, it is evident that the question: "Do I have to go to daily Mass," is outside the context of love.

Let us think for a moment. We are invited to join Christ in giving to His Father the supreme honor of total loving surrender, to share with Christ in the continuation of the redemption, to acquire more abundantly His spirit of love through the graces of sacrifice and communion. Love has only one answer: "If I can reasonably make it, I shall assist at Mass every day." This does not prevent that at times it will cost dearly to be faithful. As we have seen, it is a different thing to be united with God in the depth of our being and to overcome the impulses and moods of our nature. This very difficulty makes our surrender in love all the more pure and sincere.

Besides daily Mass there are regular oral prayers either in private or in common. The goal of these oral prayers is not merely to get them said. In this way it would be only a natural activity without any relation to the divine. It is, therefore, important that before we start praying we place ourselves in God's presence. In His presence we recite those prayers of praise, thanksgiving, mercy, and so on. When these prayers are new to us, their meaning may strike us forcefully and we would like to halt and meditate on them.

Often this is not possible. It would simply take too long. It may be useful nevertheless to return to them later in our meditation so that we can penetrate them more deeply and thus more fully allow them to increase our love for God.

As the same prayers come back regularly, we start to know them by heart. Our mind starts roaming and, though our lips formulate pious words, we may be miles away. Of course, when we notice this we try to bring our attention back to the text of our prayers but the words are like coins which have lost their imprint. They don't have any impact. What to do then? While it seems that in reciting these prayers we don't pay any attention we, nevertheless, do. This is clear from the fact that we turn the page when we have reached the bottom and are aware, when turning the last page, that our prayer is nearly finished. This also explains that, while we routinely recite these prayers, we are conscious that here we ask for God's mercy, there we sing God's praise. The means now to return to God's presence is not to let our minds wander but to penetrate more deeply these snatches we are aware of. In a quiet peaceful way we stay with them as long as they enable us to be with God. It is no longer the specific sentences that open us to God but the overall meaning of a passage, a psalm, a reading. Thus we individualize our oral prayer according to our actual spiritual condition and need. As through spiritual growth our condition keeps changing, we shall discover always new perspectives that can unite us to God.

Here again, we shall not be able to avoid all distractions. There may be days when all we do during our prayer is to attempt to orient ourselves to God over and over again. Don't be discouraged. This unrelenting but *peaceful* effort manifests to God all the more the sincerity of our love. Our dedication is purified when we continue our attempt not in order to get personal satisfaction but simply because we love Him.

Spiritual reading may also be an important aid in our spiritual ascent to God. We all become aware at times that we have exhausted our spiritual perspectives. Whatever point we touch, it is all stale and unable to help us orient ourselves to God. Spiritual reading may then be of great assistance in breaking this vicious circle. We get new perspectives and unknown horizons are opened. But only under the condition that we do *spiritual* reading. The goal of spiritual reading is to provide inspiration and not to collect intellectual knowledge or historical facts. Its purpose is to be a means of spiritual growth and deepening. To make it fruitful we must, just as with prayer, start by putting aside our worldly cares and interests. Implicitly or explicitly we place ourselves in

God's presence and then quietly and peacefully allow what we read to penetrate our deepest self. When we find a passage that strikes us as meaningful we should stay with it and gently dwell on it as long as it has something to say. In this way we may not cover very much but that is not important. The goal of this reading is not to finish a book as fast as possible but to give us spiritual nourishment As long as such reading brings us closer to God, it fulfills its purpose.

What should we read? It is evident that the gospels should be used regularly but we must be careful that we do not start to indulge in exegetical studies. These studies are, of course, valuable but they should not take the place of spiritual reading. Quietly read the text as it is and try to listen to what God has to say through His inspired word. You will discover that in a text you have read already many times you suddenly find an inspiration that brings home in a new way God's love and your dependency and weakness.

There are other books, whether they are the lives of the saints or so-called spiritual books. It is rather unimportant what book we choose as long as it can bring us closer to God and not merely fill our mind with learning. We must, moreover, not hesitate to put a book aside when we find another that better suits our actual needs.

The spiritual exercises we have considered until now have only one purpose: to unite us more intimately with God so that His lived presence becomes more and more our central concern and value. To the degree that He is the dominating factor in our hierarchy of values, we shall be able to discover His love and goodness in the world of our daily work. This then in turn will become an aid in our search for true spirituality. Once intimacy with God starts radiating not only in our personal lives but also in our work, we shall be true witnesses of the possibility, the value and the joy of living our religion.

We have all experienced that it demands a continuous struggle to prevent our work from turning from a window unto God to an obstacle to living in His presence. Even when we take the necessary precautions, we shall discover occasionally that we have become caught. This in itself is nothing to be wondered at, nor a reason for discouragement. It is merely part of the human condition. As long as we are ready to make the necessary corrections, once we discover our deviation, no lasting harm is done. These mistakes, then, can serve as a new stimulus to cling closer to God without whom all our efforts are of no avail.

We should try to have as far as possible regular working hours so that we can determine also regular times for our spiritual exercises. Leaving the working hours to our impulses will result in making them always longer because we are never really finished. Our spiritual practices are then merely squeezed in and done hurriedly if they are done at all. It is so easy to find an excuse to skip them for just this one time. The only trouble is that tomorrow the same excuse will be still more convincing. There is s-o-o-o-o much to be done. Before we know it we have become negligent and it is then doubly hard to come back to regularity.

Another precaution is to limit our work load to what we can prudently handle. It is unfortunate that still too many times the value of a person as religious is measured by the amount of work she can handle. In this atmosphere the way is open to subtle seduction. "If you want to be a good religious you have to do a lot of work and the more you do the better religious you are." In this way too many religious become totally work-oriented. They feel guilty when even for one hour they have not worked but quietly read a book or enjoyed a walk in the garden. In order to live a spiritual life we must live a human life. We shall not be able to be present to God in a peaceful relaxed way (and only in this way can we be really open to Him) unless in our daily life we learn to relax. It is, therefore, absolutely necessary that each religious has sufficient time for sleep as well as for personal relaxation. When we are always on the go, when we are always running, and sometimes very literally running, we simply cannot acquire the relaxed attitude required to be peacefully in God's presence and to be united with Him. Only when we have learned to set our work aside and are *able to just be* shall we be inspiring witnesses for the beauty and the joy of spiritual life.

The work load one can handle is not the same for all. Our physical and psychological strength is different. Some will be extremely happy when they have completed the day's regular task. It is not that they are lazy but their physical and emotional strength is less. Others may be able to take care of two jobs and still be so fresh and relaxed that they do not have any special difficulty to meet God in prayer and recollection. There is no reason for the latter to think that they are better religious. They are better workers. The quality of one's spiritual life is not determined by the amount of work she can handle but by her union with God.

This does not mean that we don't have to work hard. Religious life is not licence to laziness. Once we learn to see the guidance of God in our daily life, we realize that the will of God for me is manifested specifically in the task I have to do. *There* is where He wants me to work and witness. Because I love Him I put my whole self into it and do the best I can.

Some people have the strange notion that when they put their whole self into the work they are called to do, they do wrong because they lose their presence of God. If they mean the explicit presence of our mental prayer, they are perfectly correct. But this special union cannot be maintained the whole day. We would not be able to fulfill our task properly. When I approach my work out of love of God, when I do the best I can for His sake, my fundamental orientation effects that I am implicitly present to Him. He is present in the background as the inspiriting and sustaining force. If one would ask me why I do the best I can in my work, the spontaneous answer would be: "Because God wants me to do so."

It takes time to acquire and deepen this fundamental orientation. As our spiritual life becomes more grounded in Him, we shall discover that slowly but steadily this attitude grows into a second nature.

Occasionally, of course, we shall be carried away and fall victim to that contagious disease which is "work-fever." What do you want? We are good-willing but weak human beings inclined to all the faults of the human race. The important thing is that, when we discover the first traces of this disease, we stop working at the first occasion we have. We should then *quietly and peacefully* reorient ourselves to God. Thus quieted down we gently go to work again. Especially in such a condition we should keep to our regular working hours, unless there is a true necessity to exceed them. We then have the time and leisure to get a hold on ourselves so that after a good night's sleep and some relaxation we can dominate our work instead of our work dominating us.

In the past the decision where God wanted us to work was not left to the individual religious. We were assigned a task and that was it. If we thought that we would be better at some other function, we could present our reasons to the authorities but if they were against any change there was not much we could do. Since the renewal, however, the choice of a career is mostly left to the individual provided it fits in the concrete situation of the community. This last condition is important. Suppose a religious feels that she is called to do social work among the Eskimos in the arctic circle. This may be a beautiful vocation but if the community has no works north of Boston she will have to join another community that works in the arctic circle. If on the other hand she is convinced that her place is in her present community she cannot be called to this kind of work.

We must be very careful in deciding to what career we are called. Even when we take into account the concrete situation of the community, we still may make a serious mistake. Many communities now extend their apostolate to the socially deprived. Normally such a work starts out as an experiment where a few sisters, who feel called to this work, are allowed to settle among these people and help them in their misery. It is perfectly normal that, if they are really called to this work, they feel at home and are full of enthusiasm. The danger is that in their enthusiasm they start considering their work as the only truly apostolic work religious should do. It is then nearly inevitable that they start playing the subtle game of seduction. "Sure, teaching in school is a good work, but when you look close at it, it is evident that it is really not what Christ came to do. He helped the poor people and we as close followers of Christ, as religious, should only do this kind of work."

Though they don't say it, what they really mean is that all those who do other work are only second rate religous. They, who work for the socially deprived, they are the true followers of Christ. They may succeed in making the other religious feel guilty. Though the others may not be called at all to do this work, they become more and more insecure, especially when in their own work they experience difficulties. If this pounding goes on, they may end up *thinking* that they too are called to work with the socially deprived. They do not realize that they are merely swept off their feet by the current wave of enthusiasm and consider this, incorrectly, as a true calling. If they insist and are allowed to join this work, they undertake a task to which they are not truly called and may become unhappy.

In deciding where our future lies we must be careful. We must pray and consult others so that we may truly follow the path to which God has called us and not merely that which is now most popular. We must always remember that no one career is *by itself* excluded from the witnessing apostolate of the religious as everywhere the world needs these witnesses. When we keep this in mind we can quietly choose the career possible to us in the concrete situation. Our work can then become another path to God. At times we shall fail but that is no reason to be discouraged. All we have to do is to start again in the right direction, wiser by our mistakes and clinging closer to God because of our weakness.

TOGETHER WE STAND

WHEN the first hermits moved into the desert, they shied away from all contact with other human beings in order to live more exclusively for God alone. Normally, however, they could not hide for long. People felt attracted to them as they epitomized dedication to God. Some then moved deeper into the desert to be alone again while others stayed where they were and gathered disciples around them. They were the first beginning of communal religious life in the Church. Due to inexperience, these beginnings were often frustrating, tumultuous and difficult. It was St. Benedict who in his wisdom worked out the ground rules for religious community life and his thoughts and views have influenced practically all religious communities in the Western Church.

The advantages of communal religious life are easy to discern. The core of religious life is living in intimacy with God, growing in an always increasing love for and surrender to Him. This path of spiritual deepening is, however, fraught with many pitfalls. Man needs an experienced guide to direct, correct and encourage him in the difficulties that accompany his spiritual progress. Where can one find such an experienced guide better than in those communities which not only consider the spiritual life the center of their existence but also have effectively realized it in their daily living.

This support is of great value not just in the beginning of religious life but also later on. It is true of course that *I* have to live *my* life and that nobody can do that for me. But all those experienced in this life know that there are times when we become depressed and feel low. It is then a source of encouragement to feel that I am not alone, that I am supported by those living with me. They too experience these difficulties and, nevertheless, quietly and peacefully continue to do the best they can for the love of God. To know this is by itself already a factor that can lift up my spirits. Even if I do not speak to anyone about my troubles, I am aware that they are with me, and that we all together are before God to whom we have dedicated our lives.

We have entered a *religious* community, that is a community whose goal is to encourage, assist and support the members in their endeavor to reach a more intense living of the spiritual life. We are not a work-group whose primary aim is to take care of some common work such as a school or hospital. This common work may be present but it may also be absent. In relation to the purpose of a *religious* community this factor is of secondary importance. The dominating guiding principle of the religious community should not be the concern for how to best take care of the work but how to best promote the spiritual living of its individual members. If there ever is a question of the good of the spiritual life *or* the good of the work, the second must always give precedence to the first.

It is beyond doubt that life in community, besides its advantages, also creates difficulties. Where humans live together there are human failings. Unfortunately, these difficulties are sometimes unnecessarily aggravated by a faulty understanding of what community is.

Some people see as the ideal of community to be one big happy family. Though this view certainly has a value, it too easily idealizes the happiness of the ordinary family to unrealistic proportions and it gets into difficulty when it overlooks the hard but realistic fact that we simply are not a family. The community is composed of individuals of different background, family and education. While as times go on these differences may lose their sharp edges they can never be eliminated.

There is first the difference in each one's vital dimension. This dimension refers to our biological processes, the working of our glands, our kidneys, our blood pressure, our metabolism and all the various bodily operations which promote or hinder a healthy constitution. No two persons are totally alike organically. Each is born with this particular interaction of tensions and pulls in his bodily organs. These

[117]

factors create for each person a particular mood that is the foundation of her psychological outlook in life.[1]

I am born with my individual set of biological and emotional conditions. I did not choose them. This is the way God wanted me to be in the vital dimension. As life goes on variations are possible but this basic structure is part of the unique, irreplaceable me. In my attempt to be the one God has called me to be I have to listen to my vital dimension and remember that it is different from that of anyone else. The fact, for example, that I am able to take care of two jobs does not mean that everyone else should be able to do so. If on the other hand someone else can do much more work than I, I must accept this fact in all humility. Trying to do more than my vital dimension allows me is in fact trying to be someone I am not and is, therefore, not following the path of God's calling. I should of course do the best I can in the concrete situation but I should always respect the limits of my own vital self as well as that of others. This is sometimes painful but here too we are called to surrender to God in love, convinced that out of love for us He made us the way we are.

---

[1]The personality theory used in these pages has been developed by Adrian van Kaam, C.S.Sp., Ph.D. and worked out in the issues of *Envoy,* February through June, 1972. The same topic is considered in his book *On Being Yourself* (Dimension Books, Inc.) which at the time of this writing is at the press.

This vital dimension is not the only individually distinguishing charactertistic. I was born in a specific family with its own traditions, customs and mentality. In my most impressionable years I absorbed this particular atmosphere so deeply, though unconsciously, that it becomes indestructible. I acquired fixed ways of doing things, of meeting and treating people. I assimilated certain prejudices and established opinions which are so rooted in me that they function as a second nature. They influence me and make me act in a certain pattern without my being aware of it. In this atmosphere I also come in contact with spiritual values as they are considered and lived in my family. If in my family God and religion are only a superficial issue, this is the way I take it over, while if the spiritual values are considered fundamental factors they will be communicated to me as such. A further differentiation is the ethnic background of my family. Life and religion are viewed and lived differently in an Irish family than in a family where the dominating influence is Mexican or Italian.

As I grow I have to personalize, to make my own these various influences, customs, habits. Now I have to live them through personally and accept or reject them because I personally consider them good or harmful. Whatever personal stand I take, this earlier formation will always influence me either as an affirmation, a challenge or a reproach. In my later life I simply cannot assume new values as if the old ones never existed in me. In order to develop into a harmonious person I have to take this childhood influence into account and integrate the old and the new while at the same time eliminating what is deficient in them.

In every human being this familial-cultural self combines with the vital self. The consequence is that even though the children of the same family go through the same early formation, they are not the same because in the very assimilation and living of this formation the individual vital self influences the person.

It is as this unique vital and familial-cultural self that I have to go to God. Trying to go to God as if I were someone else is not following *my* path and, therefore, is not trying to become the person God has by His grace called me to be.

This brings us to the third individual aspect and difference in my life. I am born with a given vital self. I am formed to a familial-cultural self but this is mostly done during the years when I myself have not yet the power of discernment in this realm. When I grow up and start to live my personal life, I have to attempt with this vital and familial-cultural self to answer the call of God in my individual life. This call is specifically and individually directed to me and to no one else. It is the third individualizing and distinguishing factor.

Normally, this call of God does not reach me through revelation or any other special divine intervention. The Spirit speaks foremost to each one of us in the concrete situation in which we are. When I am appointed a teacher, in this appointment the Spirit manifests His will and calling for me. He asks me that out of love for the divine I put my whole self in this task, in this preparation, in this lecture in accordance with my vital and familial-cultural self. The more God is at the center of my existence the more I shall be able to see the divine will and my calling in this concrete work. In spiritualizing this situation as it factually is I become more the one I am called to be. Thus I fulfill God's will and become more united to Him.

From what we have said it is clear how much a religious community differs from a regular family. Each one of us is different in the vital self as well as in the familial-cultural background and each is called by God's unique will which is different for everyone. These so different people have come together to support and encourage one another in *personal* spiritual living. The purpose of the community in no way is to make them all alike. Its task is to assist each individual to become the *unique* person she is called to be. In other words, the community has to allow each member to develop into the truly unique and, therefore, different person as God conceived her to be from all eternity. It is not the community's role to eliminate these differences but to respect them and to help them develop according to God's plan.

It is to be noted that we speak here about individual distinguishing characteristics which can and should go together with a fundamental agreement. It is, for example, necessary that persons living in one community should agree on the fundamental meaning of religious life and the way it is practiced in their order. One who is here in fundamental disagreement is in the wrong place. Similarly it is necessary that the members accept the common ways of doing the common things of daily life, presence at prayer, meals, and so on. The very word "common" points to the fact that it is done commonly. This is not possible if everyone does it her own way.

Some people feel that they cannot be true individuals if they are not allowed to do their own thing even here. We touch here a fundamental though not uncommon mistake. My individuality does not consist in doing a certain activity in a peculiar distinguishing way. It is what I bring to this activity that marks and develops my individuality. When two persons do the same thing but one with interior resistance while the other sees therein the will of God, the first one will become bitter and self-centered and the second will grow spiritually. It is even quite possible that the way in which I propose to do one of these common practices is better. I should try to explain this to the others. If they are unable or even unwilling to see my viewpoint, this very fact manifests God's concrete will in the actual situation. I humbly have to accept and follow the common practice. It is the way I accept this contrariety that will stunt or promote my individual growth and spiritual development.

It is impossible to establish a happy religious community unless there is respect for each one's personality together with support and encouragement for one another to live a deep spiritual life. We are not a secular community nor a work group but a *religious* community coming together in order to better live the spiritual life. This means that in the house we live in, the convent or the monastery, we must create an atmosphere that is conducive to personal growth and spiritual deepening.

The monastery or the convent is the home to which we retire after our work in the world in order to work, live and pray peacefully and quietly before and with God. This is not possible when we throw the house open so that any visitor can come in and settle herself with some sister in any corner of the house. Not only do these visitors intrude on the privacy of the other sisters but they create the noise of the market place instead of the atmosphere of silence and recollection which are such powerful aids to our spiritual growth.

This does not mean that we should not be friendly

to our visitors and receive them graciously. But they should not be allowed in the quarters reserved for the sisters. We must never forget that our convent or monastery is not a family home. It is a home for *religious*. After being the whole day in the world and often in the center of attention, they need a place where in the privacy of their surroundings they can relax and live their personal lives without intrusion from outsiders. They must be able to find the quiet and recollection which assists them in living with God. Only when we take seriously the fact that the core and center of religious life is living with God shall we effectively attempt to create the required atmosphere in the convent or monastery.

It is beyond doubt that in certain situations the establishing of this atmosphere meets with concrete difficulties. A good number of sisters do not live in a convent proper but in a family home that was changed to a convent by merely changing the name. These homes are not exactly built to promote recollection and solitude. The situation gets worse when the sisters are crowded in a house that is too small. In these circumstances it is more difficult to have a house of recollection and silence but precisely because of the increased difficulty we should apply ourselves to this goal with greater effort. This attempt asks the cooperation of all involved but once they succeed they will appreciate the right atmosphere and know it is worth the cost.

What to do if the other community members do not cooperate? Don't get tense about it and don't be discouraged. Relax and quietly live your life as you are called to live it before God. It is true that the outward situation can be a powerful aid in living with God but a favorable condition is not an absolute requirement. Here too we must learn to discover the will of God in the actual concrete situation. If I am placed in a community where silence and recollection are absent this too falls under God's plan for me. With His grace I should attempt to live a deep spiritual life wherever I am placed. This is certainly more difficult when the circumstances are unfavorable but it is precisely in these adverse conditions that my love for God is tested and purified. At the same time this difficulty makes me cling closer to Him as I all the more realize my need for His protection and grace.

When St. Teresa lived in the Convent of the Incarnation, God called her to live according to the Carmelite rule in all its rigor. She quietly did so and reached a deep union with God. The noteworthy feature is that she never condemned her sisters for living an easier life than she did. They lived according to the light they received and sanctified themselves in that way. We must do the same. When God gives us the grace to pursue a deep spiritual life, we must be extremely grateful without, however, condemning those who take the easier way. It is quite possible that they don't observe the rule well, but, unless I am in charge, it is not for me to judge. When the legitimate authority allows them to go on as they do, all I have to do is quietly follow the light of God in my life as I am called.

In this last part we touch upon a very important but delicate and difficult point in community life. In theory we all admit that the community is meant to foster in its members personal and spiritual growth and to allow them to follow God's call by integrating their vital and familial-cultural selves in this ascent to God. In practice this means that we have to put up with each other's idiosyncracies. When we say it this way, we immediately realize that this is quite a large order. Still, only when we allow each one to be herself can we have true community life.

We all, though in varying degrees, have difficulty to bear with people who see things in a way different from ours. I implicitly assume that my way of seeing things is *the* way. Hence anyone who sees them differently sees them wrongly or at least not in the best possible way. In spite of all my talk about maturity, I have not yet reached the stage where I can quietly live my life because this is the best way *for me*. As soon as others see things in another way I feel this implicitly as an attack on me. I become insecure. Woe to the community if I am a strong person who does not rest until all the others see things my way. This is not fostering true community life but a subtle and, therefore, all the more pernicious manipulation of others.

It is a remarkable thing that when others see things in a different way my first thought is that they are wrong. It is, of course, arrogance to always think that others are wrong and never that I myself may be mistaken. But let us suppose that I am right. I try of course to make my case clear to the other. But what if she does not see my point? She may have examined the situation as carefully as I and arrived at a different conclusion. It would be absolutely wrong to start speaking about bad will, narrow-mindedness and so on. The other may simply be unable to see my point and I have to learn to accept this fact in peace and mildness. Refusing to do so not only disturbs the harmony of the community but I myself am the real loser. I become irritated, angry, self-centered, and lose the quiet way of living which is so important for spirituality.

It is also possible that the other not only sees but also does things her own way. It may be that it is not the best way but that does not mean that her way cannot succeed. Precisely because it is her way it may harmonize best with her vital and familial-cultural self. It is the way she is most acquainted with and which fits her. Forcing her to do things in a way which does not fit her personality, even if it is objectively the best way, will have worse results exactly because it is not her way of doing things.

I shall never be able to live a happy community life unless I allow each one to be herself and give up all attempts to remake her personality into what I think it should be. I simply have to give up playing God and be tolerant enought to allow others to see and do things in their way. (We of course exclude here reference to professional duties, such as teaching or nursing, where certain processes have to fit into a system and can be done only one way.)

This difference of personalities can be rather painful. Especially in a small community, I cannot but notice how different the other is; she may, therefore, irritate me. In my mind I fully accept the principle that I must allow the other to be herself and that she is different from me, but when I factually experience that she is different I often cannot be at peace with it. I must realize that, even when intellectually I see the correctness of a principle and am firmly resolved to act accordingly, I am, nevertheless, not always able to follow it through. My emotional self has its own pattern and I have no absolute control over it. Only through long and regular practice do I acquire a certain facility to make my emotional self follow what my mind sees as best.

It is not sufficient that my mind sees the truth as an abstract principle. I have to learn to assimilate it so that it becomes a deeply *lived* conviction that permeates my life. In this way this principle can slowly but steadily influence the living movements of my emotional self. In our case this means that it is not enough to admit solely in an abstract way that the other is called by God to be her unique self. The truth then remains still outside the concrete movement of my daily living. Reverence for the uniqueness of the other has to become a deeply lived conviction based upon the respect of God's plan for each of us. When this reverence is taken up and assimilated in my own life movement, it can influence my emotional life.

The trouble is that my irritation with the other often takes possession of me before I am aware of it. As few people ever totally master this difficulty, I can expect that I too will be hampered by it. What to do when the irritation takes hold of me in spite of my good will? Some people try to overcome the difficulty by bringing to their mind the good qualities of the other but normally they end up as, or even more, irritated. The reason is that my irritation is in my emotions and these are not moved by intellectual concepts. This irritation is by itself merely a natural phenomenon, neither good nor bad. The danger is that I start acting under influence of this irritation. If at all possible I must not at that moment take any action in relation to the irritating person until my irritation has quieted down. Otherwise not the reverence for God's will but my own emotionality will be the principal guiding factor in my behavior.

How does one quiet down this irritation when

every day it finds new food in the presence of the other? A first requirement is to admit that I am irritated. I have to acknowledge that at present I am not influenced by divine guidance but by my own emotions. Once I accept this fact, I must take a relaxed look at myself. This very relaxing already tends toward a diminishment of my tension. This look at myself means that my attention is diverted from the other and from what so terribly irritates me. I must then have the courage to admit that the whole thing is rather stupid. I don't want to be irritated and here I am all on fire. Why? Because I allowed the irritating factor to take a hold of me, to settle within my inner self and there it grows and grows till it becomes a mountain I cannot handle. What in itself is only a small daily incident thus develops into a drama. I have to relax and let it fall away from me, let go of it. I should do this peacefully and quietly before God who knows my weakness and I should ask Him to give me His grace to improve. When next time I feel the first twinges of my irritation, I must again in a relaxed and peaceful way let it go through me without allowing it to take root.

We emphasize that all this has to be done in a relaxed and peaceful way. If I become tense the difficulty still has a full hold on me and I may then be in for psychological difficulties. I have to learn to smile at my fumbling attempts. Even when at times I still fall in the trap, I am not amazed nor discouraged.

After all, I am only a weak human being. This very weakness urges me to come closer to God, to deepen my living in His love. Thus what, if not properly handled, can become an obstacle provides, with God's grace, a new stimulus to spiritual living.

We can describe a happy community life as a living together in charity. What is charity? Charity comes from the latin word "carus" which means something precious, something of high price. Webster refers to this in his dictionary and then says: "Charity is loving others for the sake of God."Charity consequently is love but with a special accent. As Thomas Aquinas brings out: "Charity is a perfection of love insofar as that which is loved is considered precious" S. Th. I II, 26, 3. In view of all this we may describe Christian charity as the virtue by which we love our fellow man because he is precious insofar as he is created, loved and redeemed by God.

I cannot practice this Christian charity unless I live close to God. We saw before that the meaning the world has for me depends on my personal world of meaning. If my world of meaning is a functional one, I shall see everything in a functional light in order to organize and use it for my own purpose. But if my personal world of meaning is permeated by the divine as the radiating center of my existence and the focus through which I approach the world, then reality will manifest to me its deepest ground and my fellow man will appear to me as one who is so precious that God gave His only-begotten Son to redeem him.

Charity is totally other-oriented. It does not look for a return or profit as otherwise it would not be charity but hidden self-centeredness. Charity views only the good of the other in total unselfishness. This is what makes the practice of charity so difficult. We may say to ourselves that we are not looking for gratitude or recognition but if they are not given we become easily irritated. "After all, I do not do this to receive thanks but if she were a decent person she would give at least some sign of appreciation. Instead she acts as if it is due to her." If we act in true charity this lack of recogntion will still bother us but it will not hold us back from further charitable activity.

Our charity should be universal as all men are created, loved and redeemed by Christ. This universality is possible only if we really see Christ in our neighbor so that in spite of our being hurt by ungratefulness or indiscreet demands we continue to serve Christ in the ungrateful person. Even the meanest person is still called by God and at least potentially open to His grace. But only a loving union with Christ can make us see the preciousness of such a person.

The manifestations of charity are many but they will not be true unless they are based on and permeated by care, concern and respect for the other. We must care for our neighbor. She who sees her sister desiring help but refuses to assist her, when she is able, cannot be said to have charity. But it should be an assistance full of concern. Too often the charitable activity is without heart. This especially happens when the activity is institutionalized, but it is also present in the personal charitable endeavor. We help but reluctantly. We are not really present to the other in her need. We perform the act of charity, taking care that the other realizes how kind we are in doing so. True charity possessess the difficult art of showing the other that it is a pleasure to help and in no way does it make her feel guilty. Looking beyond the perhaps repulsive qualities of the other, we eye the precious value she has before God and therefore also for us, the followers of Christ. Finally, our charity must be based on and permeated with respect for the other. In our charitable activity we must fully accept the other as she is. Only true unselfishness is able to make the receiver of our charity feel that as she is she is precious to us instead of being our debtor.

Living together in charity means that each member of the community is precious to us. This great value is not based on the amount of work she can do or on the fact that she is likeable. The foundation of Christian charity is beyond all that, rooted as it is in the very nature of being a creature, loved and redeemed by Christ. This fundamental value is present in everyone in spite of the faults, the temperamental fluctuations and individual characteristics that are manifested in daily living.

Living together in charity implies that we allow each one of the community members to be as God called her to be. True charity does not impose upon the other, does not manipulate. Too often in the name of charity we force the other to accept our advice and assistance, not aware that in spite of our good will we lack respect as well as concern. If we were present in true concern, we would perceive when she is not able or willing to accept our so-called benefits which in fact may not be much more than attempts to make her feel guilty and become dependent on us. We must realize that it may be one of the highest manifestations of charity to allow the other to be alone and quietly go *her* way. In our eyes this may not be the best way but if it is her way we must respect her calling by God.

It is possible, of course, that it is not even her way as may be apparent when, for example, she is losing the spirit of religious living. We must then be careful. If we are on good terms with that sister, we may at an opportune moment be able to broach the subject but only when we can do this peacefully and quietly in a spirit of great humility and utter unselfishness. Talking to her in an approach of self-righeousness and indignation will be experienced by her as a "butting in" on her life. The consequence will be greater stubborness. There is one thing we always can and should do for our community members and that is praying and sacrificing for them without letting them know.

If we are in charge and have to bring to her attention that she is not following the right path, we should do so only after long and sincere prayer for God's assistance as it is only through His grace that she can better her life. Our conversation should radiate our true concern and respect so that even when we have to take unpleasant measures she will know that it is not out of revenge but out of sincere interest in her.

All of us, living in community, should regularly read and meditate on St. Paul's words on charity. In his first epistle to the Corinthians he writes:

> Charity is always patient and kind,
> it is never jealous;
> charity is never boastful or conceited;
> it is never rude or selfish;
> it does not take offense and is not resentful.
> Charity takes no pleasure in other people's sins but
> delights in the truth;
> it is always ready to excuse, to trust, to hope, and to
> endure whatever comes.

13, 4-7

We see that St. Paul emphasizes mostly what we should not do: not boast, not be conceited, rude or selfish. We should not be jealous or resentful nor take pleasure in the other's faults. The advice to be patient is of great value. Charity is never in a hurry but can wait, always ready to trust, to hope and to endure *whatever* comes.

Charity consists in the readiness to be of assistance when the chance is there and the other open to it. For the rest we simply have to be there with the other, always ready, always available but never imposing. When we live in charity each one gets a chance to live *her* life and to be herself as God called her, knowing all the time that she is supported and encouraged by the other members of the community to live her personal life with God. In a community where charity prevails, there is no gossiping, no tearing the other down, no giving in to envy. Each member feels at home because she knows she is accepted as she is, strong in the confidence that even when she is not there charity prevents the others from destroying her good name. This is true community living.

In a community I visited, I met three sisters who were very enthusiastic about common bible reading. They thought that it was a beautiful thing to read the bible together and be enlightened by the comments of the various sisters present. But the other sisters of that community did not want this. "How can we have community life if we don't do this?"

It took some time before the sisters could understand that such a specific common exercise is not necessary for true community life. If all the sisters freely agree to do their bible reading in common that is fine. But if they do not want to do so, that is their privilege. Community living is living in charity, having care, concern and respect for the other and allowing each one to be herself and follow the path to which God has called her. Common bible reading may be a good thing but trying to impose this on those who do not want it, while it is not prescribed by the rule, is a lack of respect and kindness and, therefore, a lack of charity.

One may say that if community living is nothing but living together in charity then it does not mean too much or demand too much. Anyone who is of that opinion has never really tried to practice charity for one whole day. Charity is a personal attitude that covers all contacts with our fellowmen from our first sleepy "good morning" till the last "good night." In common prayer by adjusting voice and tempo to the others. At meals by passing the food and engaging in conversation that pleases the others instead of glorifying our own performance or elaborating our various aches and pains. During work by patience, kindness, understanding, unselfishness, always ready to help without showing anger or irritation, without ever imposing ourselves or manipulating the other. Anyone who has tried sincerely to live this way, not just as an interesting fad, but as a deeply lived, always attempted realization of God's love, knows that this is not an easy task. She also knows that in this way she is following Christ, who in total unselfishness willed only our good. Living in charity is working at making ourselves charitable, that is more humble, more self-effacing, more understanding. Only when our personal lives become radiated with God's love shall we be able to deepen our lived view of others as truly precious.

It is given to very few to reach perfection in charity. Most of us, ordinary stragglers on the road to God, will have to be satisfied with a slow improvement interspersed with failure. But this is the way we are and no reason to be discouraged. Instead of becoming depressed by our deficiencies, we must turn to God and make of these mistakes a new stimulus to come closer to Him, who alone through His grace can bring us to the degree of perfection He has called us to.

THE HIDDEN LIFE

BY my pro-
fession I have chosen to make God the center of my
existence. Living with Him in the intimacy of my
inner self is the main concern of my life to which all
other factors take second place and from which they
all acquire their fundamental meaning. This living
with God is only possible if I allow Him to enter my
life not merely as a concept but as a person with
Whom I am in a personal relationship. In this personal
interaction we are unequal partners. God is the source
of my existence and my salvation. In infinite love He
eyes only my good in the pattern of life He has
conceived about me from all eternity. I, on the other
hand, am the one who is redeemed and graced and
who by His mercy has been called to the religious life.

Living in the intimacy of God requires that I
surrender to Him in a loving and total dedication by
which I open to Him an unlimited credit and absolute
trust. By this surrender I give God a free hand to
guide my life to whatever He sees as good for me,
convinced that in my weakness and lack of insight I
can never find and walk the path to the true
happiness to which I aspire.

Thus I become a true imitator of Christ who said
of Himself "My aim is to do not My own will but the

will of Him who sent Me" John 5, 30. No wonder
that the life of Jesus has been the constant inspiration
of all those who in religion attempt to follow Him
more closely. Through the centuries the gospels have
been the trusted guide to intimacy with Jesus. There I
contemplate Him walking through His native country,
calling His disciples, speaking to the crowds. They
place in front of me the good Shepherd as He heals
the sick, consoles those in sorrow and receives the
children. I see how through His miracles He acquires
the acclaim of the crowd but inflames the hostility of
His enemies. Even when He knows that they are
planning to take His life, He continues His ministry,
undaunted by danger, because it was the will of His
Father that He should pursue His calling. This will of
the Father He followed till the end, where, left by His
followers, He offered His life for me in the agony and
the pain of the cross.

Meditating on the gospels I listen to the words of
Christ as directed to me and I contemplate Him as He
travels through the villages and hamlets. But these
external circumstances are only the framework in
which I try to come in contact with His inner
attitudes. The external situation is a guide that can
lead me to a deeper understanding of the spirit by
which He was animated. It is not the concrete
situation which I am called to recreate in my life but
Christ's inner attitude, His kindness, His love, His
patience and goodness and above all His dedication to

the will and the glory of His Father. It is these inner attitudes which I have to imitate in my personal life assisted by His grace.

This is an important point to remember as the actual circumstances of my life are far different from those of Christ as He wandered through Palestine. His task was to kindle the fire and to bring to its warmth as many as possible. Thus He spoke to the masses and became a public figure. During the last few years of His life He became the center of attention, evoking waves of enthusiasm but also of hatred. He was the object of conversation on the roads and around the fire. He became the lone protagonist, seen as a threat to the power of the high priest and his associates. As He followed His path with absolute fidelity, His career came to a climax when His enemies saw His elimination as the only solution. Little did they surmise that in condemning Him to death they were unconscious collaborators in the fulfillment of God's plan and the redemption of mankind.

Next to this tempestuous climax the life of the ordinary religious looks pale. After her formation is finished she starts to work at her professional job. She is a teacher, a nurse, a social worker or whatever professional task she is qualified for. She works in various places, thirty, forty, fifty years until she dies or retires. Her name may be in the paper when she makes her profession or has her silver or golden jubilee. For the rest she is unknown outside the small circle wherein she moves. No crowds gather to hear her. She has no army of followers nor of enemies. Normally her death is uneventful with only a few people aware that she has returned to God to Whom she had dedicated her whole life. If the local newspaper has an active reporter there may be a short notice in the next edition but that is all. When she entered the convent, she left the world behind and the world did not take long to forget her.

This absence of notoriety does not prevent the religious from living a rich, full and meaningful life. The true value of one's life does not depend on external recognition but on the inner attitudes with which one faces the daily life and fulfills her regular duties. These inner attitudes Christ exemplified when He did His public ministry.

But Christ's public ministry covers only a small part of His life. Besides this apostolate of two or three years there is also the hidden life, which in its external situation has much in common with the life of the average religious. It is true that these thirty years of obscurity are only alluded to in the gospels but if we collect the various data there are enough details in the picture to be an inspiration for us.

There is first the fact that such a large part of Christ's life was lived in obscurity. Humanly speaking we would have arranged things quite differently. Not only would we not have started in a forgotten corner of the world but we would have used to the full the possibilities of the wonder child. God in His wisdom arranged things differently. Thirty years of obscurity against two or three years of notoriety. These thirty years cannot have been without value. St. Luke emphasizes this when he declares that Christ increased in favor with God (2, 52). During His stay in Nazareth He was guided by the same principle that brought Him to His death, the will of His Father. He expresses this when, after being lost for three days, He tells His parents: "Did you not know that I must be busy with My Father's affairs" Lk. 2, 50. During those thirty years also He was busy with His Father's affairs, doing in obscurity the daily chores of a workman's family. These were menial jobs, but they were of immense value, not in the material sense but because of the inner attitude by which the God-Man with infinite love fulfilled the will of His Father.

This will of the Father often came to Him through the decisions of His parents. Mary and Joseph, great as they were in virtue, possessed the normal talents, which by their human nature were far below the insight, wisdom and depth of their Son. Nevertheless, "He was obedient to them" Lk. 2, 51.

To all appearances He was just an ordinary boy and young man. He was a pleasant person in favor with the people (Lk. 2, 52). For the rest there was nothing remarkable about Him. Just a boy or young man living amidst the family quarrels of the relatives and their petty jealousies. He attended the synagogue and the festive gatherings. But He remained unobtrusive. That is why later on when He had become a national and public figure they were amazed. In the little hamlet where all mothers dreamt of a great future for their sons, they were jealous at His sudden fame. "After all, He is just the Son of Joseph, that workman in the next street. We know Him and His family. How can He be so great? He never even went to the rabbinical school. How can He preach with authority?" cf. Mt. 13, 54-57. His family was shocked by His dangerous behavior and the words He uttered. So one day "they set out to take charge of Him, convinced He was out of His mind" Mt. 3, 21.

These little hints in the gospels clearly show how hidden and inconspicuous the greatest part of Christ's life was. Nevertheless, in this unobtrusive everyday life He glorified the Father fulfilling His will in the simple everyday task, performed in and with infinite love for the glory of His Father. When the moment arrived to become a public figure and to begin His public ministry that would lead to His death, He was moved by the same dedication and love that sustained Him during the thirty years He lived in obscurity as a workman's Son.

Few of us are called to bring the supreme sacrifice of our lives. The normal pattern of religious life consists in the recurrence of daily duties without any notoriety. The hidden life of Christ can thus become a powerful inspiration. It teaches us that the depth and richness of our spiritual life are not determined by the nature of our activities but by the dedication and spiritual depth we bring to our task. Not what we do is the decisive factor but, as long as it is God's will, it is the way we do it that counts.

In this perspective no activity is unimportant, be it cleaning a corridor, cooking a meal, teaching or helping the sick. Each of our activities can become an imitation of Christ and a sharing in the work of redemption, when we do it with loving surrender to God's will. But then we must be really present to the task at hand. Too often we are inclined to divide our days into worthwhile works and non-worthwhile ones. The latter we perform but we are not really with it. Our mind and our heart are ahead of themselves and occupied with what we classify as worthwhile activities. We must never forget that the will of God manifests itself in the concrete situation "now." However insignificant our work is materially, it contains God's call and invitation to manifest our love and surrender to Him "now" in *this* activity at *this* moment by applying ourselves to it wholeheartedly, though peacefully. It is in the present "now" that we are invited to live and to be present to God. Thus every activity is an important activity and every day a good day.

This attitude does not take away the hardships and difficulties of our work. They are inherent in our human condition. But this approach prevents our miseries from becoming a senseless torture without any deeper perspective. Seen in the light of faith these miseries are and remain miseries but in a loving surrender to God they are transformed into the building stones of a deeper spiritual life and a concrete imitation of Christ the Redeemer.

Such a life is only possible when I am animated with a quiet, peaceful but firm determination to truly live my religious life, which is a life of growing unselfishness in intimacy with God. Only with this gentle but decisive resolution can He become the center and core of my existence and radiate not only in my deepest self but also in my personal conduct and work. Even then I must be prepared to face incidental infidelities. As always in the spiritual life this must not discourage me. These weaknesses show just how weak I am and should urge me to come closer to God. My very infidelity is then a stimulus for greater love and fidelity to Him to Whom I have dedicated my life as a religious.